—Diseases and People—

# EBOLA VIRUS

Edward Willett

**Enslow Publishers, Inc.**

40 Industrial Road      PO Box 38
Box 398      Aldershot
Berkeley Heights, NJ 07922    Hants GU12 6BP
USA      UK
http://www.enslow.com

Howard High Media Center

# Acknowledgment

Enslow Publishers, Inc. wishes to thank Dr. Frederick A. Murphy for his help advising on the manuscript.

**Library of Congress Cataloguing-in-Publication Data**

Willett, Edward, 1959
    Ebola virus / Edward Willett.
        v. cm. — (Diseases and people)
    Includes bibliographical references and index.
    Contents: Profile — A terrifying killer — The history of ebola — What is ebola hemorrhagic fever? — Diagnosing ebola hemorrhagic fever — Treatment of ebola hemorrhagic fever — Social implications of ebola hemorrhagic fever — Preventing ebola hemorrhagic fever — Research and future prospects — Q&A — Ebola hemorrhagic fever timeline.
    Contents: Diseases and people.
    ISBN 0-7660-1595-5 (hardcover : alk. paper)
    1. Ebola virus disease—Juvenile literature. [1. Ebola virus disease. 2. Diseases.] I. Title. II. Series.
RC140.5 .W554 2003
616.9'25—dc21
                        2002010149

Printed in the United States of America

10 9 8 7 6 5 4 3

**To Our Readers:**
We have done our best to make sure that all Internet Addresses in this book were active and appropriate when we went to press. However, the author and publisher have no control over and assume no liability for the material available on those Internet sites or on other Web sites they may link to. Any comments or suggestions can be sent by e-mail to comments@enslow.com or to the address on the back cover.

**Illustration Credits:** © Corel Corporation, pp. 77, 87; Associated Press, p. 60; Centers for Disease Control and Prevention, pp. 10, 34, 44, 73; Christine Nesbitt/Associated Press, p. 20; Enslow Publishers, Inc., pp. 6, 24; Henry Mathews/Centers for Disease Control and Prevention, p. 42; Pat Roque/Associated Press, p. 12; Sayyid Azim/Associated Press, p. 27.

**Cover Illustration:** Centers for Disease Control and Prevention (background); Pat Roque/Associated Press (inset).

# Contents

# EBOLA VIRUS

**What is it?** Ebola is a viral hemorrhagic fever. "Viral" means it is caused by a virus; "hemorrhagic" means one of its symptoms is severe bleeding; and "fever" means that it causes the body's temperature to rise. It is a severe disease that causes death in 90 percent of cases.

**Who gets it?** Ebola affects men and women of any age. It also infects nonhuman primates (monkeys and chimpanzees). Confirmed cases of the disease have been reported in the Democratic Republic of the Congo (which used to be called Zaire), Gabon, Sudan, the Ivory Coast, and Uganda. No case of the disease in humans has ever been reported in the United States, but a laboratory worker in England became ill as a result of an accidental needle-stick.

**How do you get it?** Ebola is caused by infection with Ebola virus, named after a river in the Democratic Republic of the Congo in Africa located in the region where the disease was first recognized. The virus is one of two members of a unique family of viruses called the Filoviridae, or filoviruses, because they look like worms under the electron microscope. (*Filo* is Latin for "worm.") Humans do not normally carry the Ebola virus; instead, it is believed that the virus normally inhabits some other animal, and the first human patient in any outbreak of the disease becomes infected through contact with such an animal. Once a human is infected, the virus can be transmitted to other humans through direct contact with the bodily fluids of the infected person or through contact with objects that have been contaminated with infected bodily fluids.

**What are the symptoms?** The symptoms of Ebola vary from patient to patient. Most patients, within a few days of becoming infected, will develop high fever, headache, muscle aches, stomach pain, fatigue and diarrhea; some patients will also develop a sore throat, hiccups, a rash, red and itchy eyes, and bloody diarrhea. Some may vomit blood. Within one week of becoming infected, 50 to 90 percent of patients suffer from chest pain, shock, and death; some go blind and bleed out through their bodily orifices before death occurs.

**How is it treated?** There is no effective treatment for Ebola. The best doctors can do is to treat the symptoms by balancing the patient's fluids and electrolytes, making sure that they are getting enough oxygen, keeping up their blood pressure, and treating any secondary infections.

**How can it be prevented?** Because it is not known which animals carry Ebola in the wild, it is difficult to prevent outbreaks—anyone could come into contact with the virus at any time. When the disease does appear, the poor social and economic conditions in the African countries where it occurs mean that hospitals and other health-care facilities, where the patients are naturally taken, actually help to spread the disease. It is important that doctors be able to recognize Ebola so that they can help prevent its spread through "barrier nursing techniques." These techniques include wearing protective clothing, using infection-control measures such as sterilizing equipment, and isolating infected patients. The goal is to prevent anyone from coming in contact with the blood or bodily secretions of any infected patient. If the patient dies, it is equally important that there be no direct contact with the body.

The Ebola virus was first identified in what is now known as the Democratic Republic of the Congo.

# 1
# A Terrifying Killer

**Y**ambuku is a village in the Democratic Republic of the Congo, located in the tropical rain forests about 100 miles (161 kilometers) south of the Ebola River. In 1976, when the Democratic Republic of the Congo was still known as Zaire, Yambuku Mission Hospital, staffed by Catholic nuns, nurses and midwives, served a population of 60,000 people. The hospital was a collection of tin-roofed huts with concrete floors, housing a pharmacy, an operating room, and 120 beds. It had no electricity and a shortage of basic medical supplies.

Nearly 400 patients a day came through the hospital's out-patient clinic. The most common treatment was an injection of antibiotic. Unfortunately, the hospital did not have 400 needles a day to use. It only had a dozen or so, so the nuns used the same needles over and over. In addition, the needles were not sterilized between injections. Instead, the nuns would just swish them around in a pan of warm water.

There had never been a major problem with this way of doing things in the forty-one years the hospital had been in operation. That changed in 1976, when a teacher at the Yambuku Mission School came to the clinic suffering from a fever and other symptoms that the nurses diagnosed as malaria.

The usual treatment for malaria was a shot of chloroquine. The shot was given and the teacher was sent home. He felt better for a little while, but soon felt worse than ever. The next time he went to the hospital, he was admitted, suffering from high fever, bloody diarrhea, headache, chest pains, and nausea. He died three days later.

He was only the first. The disease he carried, which had never been seen before, killed eighteen of his family and friends. Hundreds of other people were infected when they were injected using the same needles used on him. While some people who only touched him survived, no one who contracted the disease as a result of an injection did.[1] Eventually, 280 people died from a new and terrifying disease that became known as Ebola hemorrhagic fever.[2]

## Named After A River

The "Ebola" part of the disease's name comes from the little river north of Yambuku. It is called a hemorrhagic fever because its symptoms include fever (a heightened body temperature) accompanied by hemorrhage (internal bleeding).

Ebola is caused by a type of virus called a filovirus. *Filo* is the Latin word for "worm." Under an electron microscope, filoviruses look a little like worms. There are many other hemorrhagic fevers besides Ebola, some of them caused by filoviruses, and others caused by other types of viruses.[3]

However, Ebola hemorrhagic fever has a reputation as a particularly terrible disease. At first, like many other diseases, including such common ones as influenza (the flu), Ebola causes fever, weakness, muscle pain, headache, and sore throat. However, as the disease progresses, vomiting, diarrhea, and rash develop, the kidneys and liver may stop functioning normally, and uncontrollable internal and external bleeding may develop. Patients may start to bleed from their eyes, ears, nose, and other orifices. They may also vomit blood produced by bleeding from their internal organs.[4]

Not everyone who gets Ebola dies from it, but the death rate in some outbreaks has ranged as high as 88 percent—that means almost nine out of every ten patients who contracted Ebola died from it.

There are three different species of Ebola virus that cause disease in humans. Each is named after the region where it was first identified. They are Ebola-Zaire (which caused the first outbreak and seems to have the highest death rate), Ebola-Sudan, and Ebola-Ivory Coast. A fourth species of Ebola virus, Ebola-Reston, causes disease in monkeys, but not in humans.[5]

So far, all the outbreaks of Ebola have occurred in Africa. Confirmed cases have been reported in the Democratic Republic of the Congo, Gabon, Sudan, the Ivory Coast, and

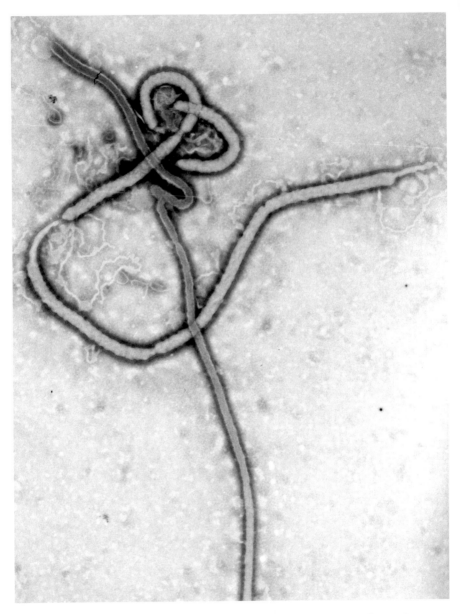

This transmission electron micrograph of the Ebola virus shows the wormlike structures of the filovirus.

Uganda. One or two isolated cases have been reported outside of Africa; for instance, a laboratory worker in England became ill after an accidental needle-stick while working with the virus, but recovered. No cases of Ebola hemorrhagic fever have ever been reported in humans in the United States.

Ebola-Reston virus, however, has caused severe illness and death in monkeys at research facilities in the United States.[6] The virus gets its name from Reston, Virginia, where it first surfaced in a group of monkeys shipped to the Hazelton Primate Center from the Philippines in 1989. Although four humans developed antibodies to the virus, indicating that they had been exposed to it, none of them became ill.[7] This outbreak became the basis of the best-selling book *The Hot Zone* by Richard Preston (New York: Random House Inc., 1994).

## The Most Dangerous Disease?

*The Hot Zone* also contributed to the popular perception of Ebola hemorrhagic fever as one of the most dangerous diseases known to man. It both is and is not. It *is* dangerous because its most virulent strain, Ebola-Zaire, kills up to nine out of ten people infected; but it is *not* as dangerous as many people think because it is relatively hard to catch and risk factors are easily controlled.

Unlike, say, influenza, which has killed millions of people over the years even though it only kills a small percentage of the people who get it, the three strains of Ebola that cause disease in humans apparently are not transmitted through the air.

The Ebola virus has caused severe illness and death in monkeys in research facilities in the United States and other countries.

Ebola is not normally present in humans. Instead, humans appear to come into contact with it by accident. That means there must be a "natural reservoir" of the virus—some animal or insect that carries it all the time and occasionally transmits it to a human. This natural reservoir has not yet been discovered by scientists.[8]

Once a human has the disease, other humans can be infected by direct contact with the blood or other bodily secretions (sweat, saliva, etc.) of the infected person. People have also been infected with Ebola through contact with objects, especially hypodermic needles, that have been in contact with infected bodily secretions.

This means that the most common avenues of transmission of the disease during an outbreak are from one family member to another (because family members care for each other, and thus come in contact with bodily fluids) or among patients, doctors and nurses in hospitals, especially hospitals where needles and syringes are reused.[9] (The transmission of disease inside a hospital is called *nosocomial transmission.*)

The fact that Ebola is transmitted primarily by close contact with bodily fluids, however, also means that breaking the chain of transmission, and thus ending an outbreak, is relatively easy. Family members and friends of infected people and medical personnel must take basic precautions that prevent contact with bodily fluids, such as wearing masks, gloves, gowns, and goggles when caring for or treating an infected person. The patient should be isolated from all uninfected, nonmedical people. Finally, everything that comes in contact with the patient should be thoroughly sterilized.

While preventing further transmission of the disease is fairly simple, there are no effective treatments for those who are infected. Instead, patients receive therapy designed to treat the symptoms and prevent fatal shock.

Preventing outbreaks from happening at all is more difficult because no one knows where in the wild Ebola lurks. The most important consideration now in preventing a single case from developing into a major outbreak is recognizing the disease so proper safety precautions can be taken. That is difficult because, as was noted earlier, Ebola looks so much like so many other diseases in the early stages.[10]

## Should You Be Worried?

Because of Ebola's reputation as a highly infectious, unstoppable killer disease (although, as has already been mentioned, it is neither all that infectious nor all that unstoppable), and because it receives so much media attention every time there is an outbreak, many people worry about the possibility of someone infected with Ebola in Africa spreading the disease to another country, such as the United States.

To understand why some people are worried—and decide whether you should be worried, too—you need to understand what Ebola is, what it does, how it is transmitted, how it can be prevented, and what the prospects are for developing an effective treatment for it.

You will learn all that and more in the next few chapters.

# 2

# The History of Ebola

Ebola hemorrhagic fever was not named until 1976, but that does not mean that other cases had not surfaced long before that. In fact, some historians suggest that a plague of Ebola may have helped to bring about the end of the Golden Age of Greece.

The plague, described in detail by the Athenian writer Thucydides, swept across the eastern Mediterranean and struck Athens three times, in 430, 429, and 427–426 B.C., at the height of the Pelopennesian War between Sparta and Athens.

At the time, Athens was much more crowded than usual because all the people from the outlying countryside had been brought into the city to protect them from attack by the Spartans. The plague killed large numbers of people, possibly including Pericles, leader of the Athenians; it has been estimated that between a quarter and a third of the population died.[1]

Thucydides, who contracted the disease but survived, said it originated in Ethiopia and spread through Egypt and Libya before falling on Athens. He said the symptoms included fever and redness and burning of the eyes, and that the inside of the mouth turned bloody-looking. He also said that the breath turned foul-smelling and that after that came sneezing, hoarseness, coughing, bilious vomiting, and an "empty heaving." The flesh turned red and livid and broke out in blisters and ulcers. Victims suffered from unquenchable thirst and high fevers. Most died on the seventh or ninth day. Others died later of weakness after extreme diarrhea. Anyone who cared for the sick or even visited them caught the disease, Thucydides wrote.[2]

Many of those symptoms also plague modern Ebola victims. The "empty heaving" sounds odd, but it is possible that the Greek phrase could also be translated as "hiccups"—and 15 percent of Ebola patients in the outbreak of Ebola in Kikwit, Democratic Republic of the Congo, in 1995 also suffered from hiccups.[3]

So, was the Plague of Athens the first recorded outbreak of Ebola? We may never know for certain. While Ebola may be one possibility, other theories include bubonic plague, dengue fever, influenza, measles, and (most recently) typhus fever.[4]

## First Modern Outbreak

What is certain is that the first outbreak of Ebola in modern times took place in Yambuku, a village in the tropical rain forests of the northern part of the Democratic Republic of the Congo (then called Zaire), in 1976.

The outbreak began when a teacher at the Yambuku Mission School came to the Yambuku Mission Hospital suffering from an illness that was first diagnosed as malaria. He was given an injection and sent home. The needle used to give him a shot was reused many more times on some of the 400 or so patients that came through the hospital every day, without being properly sterilized between uses.

The teacher came back with much worse symptoms and soon died, as did eighteen of his family and friends and hundreds of other people infected through the reuse of unsterilized needles. The final death toll was 280, or 88 percent of the 318 cases reported.[5]

No one knew at first what was killing people. The hospital closed on September 30, 1976, just twenty-nine days after the teacher received his injection. By that time, eleven of the seventeen staff members had the mysterious disease. On October 18, 1976, the World Health Organization formed an international commission to investigate. Research teams were mobilized on October 30, but by that time, the outbreak had burned itself out. The last case died on November 5.[6] Ironically, because most of the infections took place within the hospital, closing the hospital played the largest role in ending the outbreak.[7]

## "Unlike Anything Ever Documented"

Although the outbreak took place in Yambuku, the realization that its victims were suffering from a previously unknown disease took place thousands of miles away in Belgium. Dr. Peter Piot was training in microbiology at the time at the Institute for Tropical Medicine in Antwerp. Dr. Piot and his colleagues received samples of liver tissue and blood from a nun who had worked, and died, at Yambuku Mission Hospital.

"The diagnosis was yellow fever, but when we grew a culture we saw it was very different from yellow fever virus," Dr. Piot said. "The Centers for Disease Control and Prevention in Atlanta confirmed that the virus was unlike anything that had ever been documented. The next day I caught a plane to Zaire to join an international team that was investigating the outbreak. We had no clue to what had caused it."[8]

One of the people at the Centers for Disease Control and Prevention (CDC) who confirmed that the virus was unknown was Dr. Frederick A. Murphy. When Dr. Murphy put a sample from Zaire in an electron microscope on October 13, 1976, he expected to see the Marburg virus—and that is what he thought he saw. After disinfecting the room in which he had prepared the specimen, he shot photographs. According to Dr. Murphy:

> I went back to the microscope and called Karl Johnson and Patricia Webb to take a look. I shot a cassette of pictures with wet negatives not good for the enlarger and I made prints, which were available within minutes. I carried these dripping prints to the office of the Director of the CDC. It was very dramatic.[9]

The photographs revealed that in fact the virus was not Marburg, but something entirely new.

The new disease was called Ebola, after the little river 100 miles (161 kilometers) north of Yambuku; but in fact, the outbreak there was not the only one underway.

## A Second Strain Appears

Ebola also broke out in the towns of Nzara and Maridi and the surrounding area in Sudan in 1976—in fact, that outbreak actually occurred *before* the one in Yambuku. On June 27, 1976, a worker in the Nzara Cotton Manufacturing Factory cloth room became ill; he died in the Nzara hospital on July 6, 1976. A second man who worked in the cloth room died in the hospital on July 14; a third man became ill on July 18 and died on July 27, after several short stays in the hospital. He, in turn, appears to have infected many others—69 percent of the cases in the resulting outbreak were traced back to him.[10] In all, 284 cases were eventually identified. However, the strain of Ebola virus causing those cases turned out to be different than the one in Yambuku, and not quite as deadly. The death rate was 53 percent instead of 88 percent. Once again, the disease was spread mainly inside the hospital.[11]

Ebola-Sudan, as this strain of the disease was dubbed, popped up again in Nzara in 1979. Thirty-four people became ill; twenty-two of them died. Once again, every case could be connected back to someone employed at the Nzara Cotton Manufacturing Factory.[12]

No one was able to learn much about Ebola hemorrhagic fever during the first few outbreaks. Efforts were made to find the reservoir—it was presumed that the animals carried the virus in the wild—but without success.

## Ebola Enters the United States

The next time Ebola surfaced, it was not in Africa. Instead, it showed up in the United States in monkeys imported from the

Most outbreaks of the Ebola virus are linked to an unusual number of dead monkeys, chimpanzees, gorillas, or other animals. As shown here, monkeys are often sold as food by villagers. People may become infected with the Ebola virus when they eat the meat of the dead animal.

Philippines. This outbreak, first discovered at Hazleton Research Products' Reston Primate Quarantine Unit in Reston, Virginia, became famous as the subject of the book *The Hot Zone* by Richard Preston.

One hundred cynomolgus macaques from Ferlite Farms in Mindanao, Philippines, were quarantined in Reston on October 4, 1989. (United States law requires all primates imported into the country to be quarantined for thirty days, to ensure that they are free of disease.) All 100 monkeys were placed in the same room, Room F.

Any transcontinental shipment of animals tends to result in a number of deaths, but many more of the monkeys in this shipment died than would ordinarily have been expected. The staff veterinarian examined some of the dead monkeys and concluded they had died of a disease called simian hemorrhagic fever (SHF), which is similar to Ebola but does not infect humans.

However, he sent samples of the tissue to the United States Army Medical Research Institute of Infectious Diseases (USAMRIID) and euthanized all of the monkeys in Room F to prevent the possible spread of the disease. USAMRIID confirmed the presence of SHF in the samples, but euthanizing the monkeys did not solve the problem. More monkeys in a different room (Room H) died, and the disease no longer looked very much like SHF in the way it progressed or the way it spread. That was confirmed by USAMRIID, which, as it continued to examine the dead monkey tissue, eventually found the Ebola virus present in addition to SHF.[13]

The Room H monkeys had arrived in Reston on November 8, eight days before the Room F monkeys were euthanized. Both shipments came from Ferlite Farms in the Philippines, which, investigators later discovered, was experiencing a hemorrhagic fever outbreak at the same time. The question was, did the Room H monkeys catch the virus from the Room F monkeys (which would mean that the Ebola virus was transmitted through the air, rather than by close contact—something that would make it far more dangerous), or were they already harboring the virus, without showing symptoms, when they arrived?

In *The Hot Zone*, which became a best-selling book and has influenced everyone's view of Ebola as one of the world's most dangerous diseases, Richard Preston concluded that the virus was transmitted through the air, a conclusion with which most other sources agree. However, the Centers for Disease Control and Prevention does not go that far; it says only that Ebola-Reston "may" have been transmitted through the air.[14]

On November 29, the Centers for Disease Control and Prevention and the Virginia Department of Health, along with USAMRIID, decided to euthanize all the remaining animals in Room H to prevent the disease from spreading to other monkeys in the facility and possibly to the human staff. On November 30, around 500 monkeys were euthanized.

Tests of the staff revealed that four humans had developed antibodies to Ebola, indicating they had been infected, but none of them became ill. The strain infecting the monkeys appeared to be different from either Ebola-Zaire or Ebola-Sudan, and fortunately seemed less dangerous to humans. It was named Ebola-Reston.

Ebola-Reston turned up again in monkey quarantine facilities in the United States in Philadelphia (at about the same time as the outbreak in Reston) and in Texas (a couple of months later). All the monkeys involved came from the Ferlite Farms in the Philippines, but no human who was exposed to the virus, either there or in the United States, became ill.

## Another Strain Appears

A fourth strain of Ebola surfaced in Tai National Park in Côte d'Ivoire (Ivory Coast) in 1994. This time, the victims were members of a wild troop of chimpanzees being studied by scientists. In October and November of 1994, twelve members of the troop died. Autopsies of some of the dead chimps revealed damage to the internal organs similar to those of human victims of Ebola. The Pasteur Institute confirmed that diagnosis.

Researchers noted that the deaths corresponded to a time when the chimpanzees were hunting and eating Western Red Colobus monkeys, and those who ate the most meat were the most likely to die. As a result, they suspect the monkeys were carrying the virus, which turned out to be a new strain of Ebola, now called Ebola-Ivory Coast.

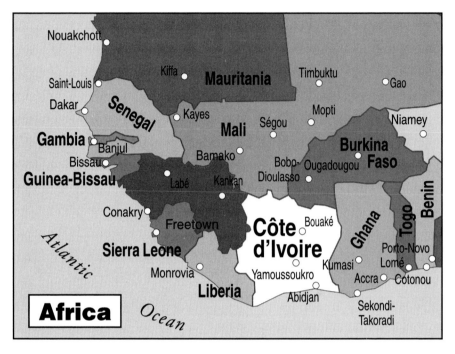

The strain of Ebola found in Côte d'Ivoire may cause disease in humans, but is not as deadly as Ebola-Zaire or Ebola-Sudan.

Ebola-Ivory Coast does cause disease in humans, but it may not be as deadly to humans as Ebola-Zaire and Ebola-Sudan. One of the scientists who autopsied one of the dead chimps became ill eight days later. She was transported to Switzerland for treatment, and recovered. No one else was infected, even though strict quarantine procedures were not followed.[15]

## Zaire Suffers Again

By 1995, sixteen years had passed since there had been a major outbreak of Ebola affecting humans. Suddenly it surfaced again, once again in Zaire, once again in a hospital, once again with deadly effects.

This time, the center of outbreak was Kikwit, a city of 500,000 people.[16] On April 6, 1995, a thirty-six-year-old laboratory technician named Kimfumu, who worked at the Mama Mobutu Maternity Hospital, fell ill with a fever. Two days later, he was admitted to hospital. Doctors originally thought he had typhoid. Then his stomach became distended, which made them think he had a perforated intestine, which required an immediate operation. They transferred him to Kikwit General Hospital, which had the facilities for operations, and on April 10, he was operated on by two doctors and two nurses. They removed his appendix and he seemed to get better, but then his stomach became even more bloated, and a second operation was performed. This time, they found that his abdominal cavity was filled with blood, because his internal organs were leaking fluids and blood into it. The doctors and nurses were spattered with Kimfumu's blood. Kimfumu went into shock and died on April 14.

Soon, members of the operating team began dying, and news of an outbreak of Ebola in Zaire made it into the outside world.[17] Thanks to the popularity of *The Hot Zone* and other books, Ebola was a hot topic. The media flooded Kikwit. Television, newspapers, and magazines were filled with stories about the outbreak.

Scientists also poured into Kikwit. They found that the outbreak had actually begun long before Kimfumu became ill.

The first case, or "index case," was a thirty-five-year-old charcoal maker and manioc farmer named Gaspar Menga. Menga cultivated a manioc, or cassava, plot and made charcoal about eight or ten miles (thirteen or sixteen kilometers) from Kikwit in the Pont Mwembe forest. On January 6, 1995, he developed a fever, bloody diarrhea, and abdominal pain. He was diagnosed at Kikwit General Hospital with a bacteria-caused abdominal disease called shigella, a fairly common ailment in the region. But by January 13 he had died, and soon so had almost every member of his family.

Funerals in the region were traditionally open-casket, and it was also traditional for family members to put their hands on the body during funerals as a last gesture of affection and farewell. Menga's wife, Bebe, his brother, Bilolo, and his uncle, Philemond, all touched the body—and all were dead by the end of January.

That wave of deaths led to a second wave—sisters, sons, daughters, and grandmother—in February, then a third wave, culminating in the death of another grandmother on March 3 in an outlying village.[18]

For some reason, that part of the outbreak died out at that point; no more cases were reported from it. However, a friend of the Menga family was admitted to Mama Mobutu Maternity Hospital and died there on March 3. There were two other deaths there in March and, at the beginning of April, six more. Kimfumu probably caught the disease during his work as a laboratory technician; the other lab technician,

26

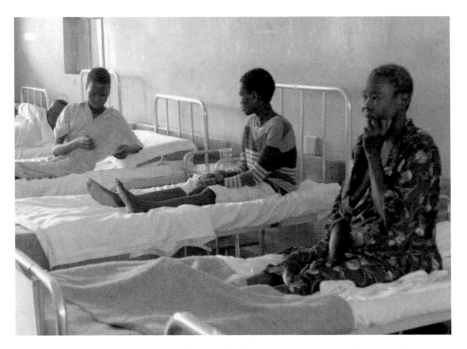

People who are infected with the Ebola virus are quarantined within the hospital.

Bienge, had actually entered the hospital the day before Kimfumu and died on the same day.[19]

Although he was not the true "Patient Zero" of the outbreak, Kimfumu was the one who brought the disease to Kikwit General Hospital. Just as in the first Ebola outbreak in 1976, the hospital became the focal point of the subsequent infections and deaths. Patients would enter the hospital and infect family members and hospital staff, who would then leave the hospital and infect other people, then return to the hospital as patients and continue the cycle.[20]

27

The Centers for Disease Control and Prevention specialists who arrived on the scene to attempt to halt the outbreak had difficulty convincing infected people to come to the hospital, because it had become so closely associated in people's minds with death. Some people hid themselves away rather than be taken to the hospital.[21] That made stopping the outbreak much more difficult than it would otherwise have been, but eventually quarantining patients and proper safety procedures stopped the chain of transmission. The final tally of the outbreak was 315 confirmed human cases and 255 deaths—an 81 percent fatality rate.[22]

As in 1976, scientists searched the forest for the natural reservoir of the virus—and as in 1976, found nothing.

## Two Outbreaks in Gabon

Two smaller outbreaks of Ebola-Zaire occurred in Gabon the following year. In the first outbreak, a chimpanzee found dead in the forest was butchered and eaten by a group of people out searching for food. Nineteen people who were involved in butchering the chimpanzee became ill; the remaining eighteen cases in the outbreak were among their family members. Twenty-one people, or 57 percent of the cases, died.[23]

In the second outbreak, a hunter who lived in a forest camp became infected and spread the disease to others. In all, sixty people became infected and forty-five of them died. Interestingly, a chimpanzee may have also been involved in that outbreak; a dead chimp found in the forest was discovered to have been infected with Ebola. A medical professional who treated Ebola patients in Gabon became ill after traveling to Johannesburg, South Africa. He survived, but a nurse who took care of him in South Africa died. No one else was infected.[24]

## A Glimmer of Understanding

After the Kikwit and Gabon outbreaks, researchers continued their efforts to discover how the Ebola virus carries out its gruesome work. In July 2000, researchers at the U.S. National Institutes of Health (NIH) and the Centers for Disease Control and Prevention, led by Dr. Gary Nabel of the NIH's Vaccine Research Center, identified the major gene in the Ebola virus that kills cells, and the protein produced by that gene that causes blood vessels to leak in an infected person. This could lead to effective drugs to counteract Ebola.[25]

Just two months later, the largest-ever outbreak of Ebola began in Uganda. This time the strain was Ebola-Sudan. As well, this outbreak was different in that Uganda had more modern hospital facilities than the Democratic Republic of the Congo. As a result, most of the transmission of the disease happened within the community rather than in the hospital (although many health workers died before proper safety procedures were put in place).

A particular problem in this outbreak was the local practice of family members ritually bathing a body after its death, then washing their hands in a communal basin. As a result, many families were entirely wiped out by the virus.[26]

The outbreak might have been far worse if not for efforts by the Ugandan government to contain it. Approximately 5,600 people who had been in contact with patients were identified and kept under observation for twenty-one-day periods by 150 trained volunteers. Efforts to educate the public and local medical workers about the importance of proper safety procedures while dealing with victims of the disease were also important.[27]

Eventually, 425 cases of Ebola hemorrhagic fever were confirmed and 225 people died, a death rate of 53 percent.[28] Researchers once again began searching for the natural reservoir of the virus, so far without success.

But even while the Ugandan outbreak was still raging, more scientific advances were being made in the fight against Ebola.

In October, a team of German and American researchers from the Mount Sinai School of Medicine in New York and Philipps Universitat in Marburg, Germany, announced that another protein produced by Ebola-infected cells actually disabled the normal production of interferon, a substance the immune system uses to kill virus-infected cells—offering another possible target for new drugs or a vaccine.[29]

## Hope For a Vaccine

And then, just a month later, news appeared in the science magazine *Nature* that researchers at the Centers for Disease Control and Prevention had created a vaccine that prevented four macaque monkeys deliberately infected with Ebola from contracting the disease.[30]

That is where we stand as of this writing. No one knows when or where the next outbreak of Ebola will occur. We know a little bit more about how the virus works, but we still have no way of effectively treating the disease. And we still do not know where in the wild the Ebola virus lurks.

Perhaps it is no wonder people are frightened of Ebola, even though it has caused relatively few deaths over the past twenty-five years. We know very little about it—and people are often fearful of what they do not understand.

# 3

# What is Ebola Hemorrhagic Fever?

In early September 2000, Esther Owete, a thirty-six-year-old woman from Kabedo-Opong in northern Uganda, began complaining of "a coldness in her body." Next came pains in the muscles in her legs, then pain in her chest. Then, she developed a fever and began vomiting blood.

"We thought it was malaria," remembered a neighbor, Justin Okot. Owete was taken to a clinic in the nearby town of Gulu, where she was injected with the antimalarial drug chloroquine and sent home.

But Owete did not have malaria, and chloroquine did not help. "She did not even last twenty-four hours," said Okot.

Her family did not last much longer. Minutes after Owete died, her neighbors reported, Owete's upset mother called for Owete's one-year-old son Sam to "suck your mother's last milk so you too can die. There is no one here to look after you now." He died four days later. Owete's mother died on October 1. Her three sisters and a nephew died soon after. In all, seven family members died in just over three weeks.

Owete was one of the first victims of an outbreak of Ebola hemorrhagic fever that eventually killed 225 people.

# Definition of Ebola

Ebola hemorrhagic fever is a severe, often-fatal disease that occurs in humans and nonhuman primates (monkeys and chimpanzees). It is caused by infection with Ebola virus, one of two members of a family of viruses called the *Filoviridae* because they look wormlike under the electron microscope. The other member of the family, Marburg virus, also causes a hemorrhagic fever (a disease characterized by both fever and uncontrolled bleeding).

Viruses are essentially just a bit of genetic material—RNA, in the case of Ebola—wrapped up inside a coat of protein. They are not, strictly speaking, alive, and they are incredibly tiny: a million viruses put together would be about the size of a speck of dust. However, the genetic material they carry inside is a code for making new copies of themselves.

Viruses, however, cannot replicate on their own. Instead, they take over the machinery of a living cell. Cells are essentially factories for turning out things like hormones, enzymes, and proteins. Viruses hijack these factories so that the cell, instead of producing what it is supposed to produce, turns out new copies of the virus. The process sometimes kills the cell; at the very least, it is bad news for the body the cell inhabits

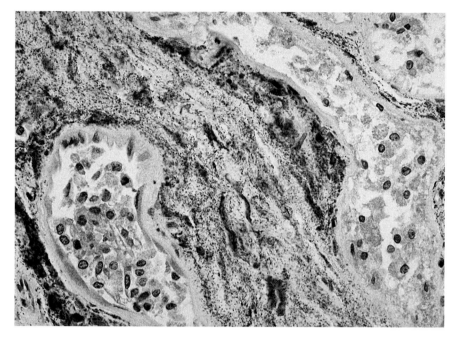

Close-up view of the Ebola virus antigen in the skin. Antigens are substances that cause the body to produce antibodies to counteract them to fight an illness or disease.

because the cell is no longer turning out the vital products it used to produce.[1]

There are four known species of Ebola virus, each named after the place where it was first discovered: Ebola-Zaire, Ebola-Sudan, Ebola-Ivory Coast, and Ebola-Reston. Only Ebola-Zaire, Ebola-Sudan, and Ebola-Ivory Coast cause disease in humans; Ebola-Reston only causes disease in nonhuman primates.

It is believed that the virus normally lives in unknown animal hosts in Africa, only sporadically infecting the human population. (Ebola-Reston is the only one of the four known species that seems to originate outside Africa. The monkeys in which it was first identified were all shipped to the United States from the Philippines.)

To date, confirmed cases of Ebola hemorrhagic fever have been reported in the Democratic Republic of the Congo (formerly Zaire), Gabon, Sudan, the Ivory Coast, and Uganda. A single case of an individual whose blood showed antibodies to the disease, indicating that he may have been infected even though he did not become sick, has been reported in Liberia, and a laboratory worker in England became ill with Ebola hemorrhagic fever (but recovered) after accidentally sticking himself with a contaminated needle. No case of the disease has ever been reported in humans in the United States, although Ebola-Reston has caused severe illness and death in monkeys in research facilities here. Several research workers were infected with Ebola-Reston during those outbreaks, but did not become ill.

Outbreaks of Ebola hemorrhagic fever occur sporadically, and are usually spread within a hospital or other health-care setting. It is likely that occasional isolated cases that do not result in large-scale outbreaks go unreported.

Once the virus makes the jump from its unknown animal host into humans, humans can spread it to other humans in several ways. The most common method is through direct contact with the blood or other bodily secretions (sweat, saliva, vomit, etc.) of an infected person. That is why outbreaks often wipe out whole families who live in close quarters and care for each other when they are sick. People can also be exposed to Ebola virus through contact with contaminated objects, especially hypodermic needles.

Ebola-Reston may have spread among the monkeys in research facilities through the air. All Ebola virus species have been shown to have this ability under research conditions, but airborne spread has not been documented among humans in the real world in either hospitals or homes.[2]

## Symptoms of Ebola Hemorrhagic Fever

One of the most insidious things about Ebola hemorrhagic fever, as with a lot of serious illness, is that at its start, it does not seem very serious.

Like many other illnesses, including influenza, Ebola symptoms begin with fever, chills, headaches, muscle aches, and loss of appetite, usually within one to two weeks after infection. (Because these symptoms also mimic those of other tropical infections such as salmonellosis, typhoid fever, yellow fever, viral hepatitis, malaria, and others, Ebola is often misdiagnosed in the early stages, increasing the risk of the disease being passed on to others within a health-care setting.)

The initial symptoms may be followed by vomiting, diarrhea, abdominal pain, sore throat, a rash, and even severe hiccupping. Pregnant women infected with Ebola will often suffer a miscarriage.

By the fifth day of the fever (which usually runs its course in a week), bleeding begins inside the intestinal tract, sometimes resulting in vomiting large amounts of blood. The mucous membranes that line the nose and throat may also begin to leak blood. Patients may begin to bleed from every orifice in their bodies, including eyes, nose, ears, and anus, and even from puncture wounds where they have received shots or intravenous drugs.

After between six and sixteen days, the loss of blood and deterioration of the internal organs often results in death. Those patients who survive usually begin to recover after between a week and ten days, although it will often take them five weeks or more to recover completely.[3]

## "The Ones That Bled, Died"

Some descriptions of victims of Ebola talk about the patients melting away and make it sound as if blood invariably pours out of them; but that is not necessarily the case.

Philippe Calain and Pierre Rollin were two of the doctors from the Centers for Disease Control and Prevention who were sent to Kikwit, Zaire, at the time of the 1995 outbreak of Ebola there. In the General Hospital, they found and spoke to many patients suffering from the disease.

"Most of the time they said they were thirsty," Calain said. He continued:

> Not mainly because they had nothing to drink, but because one of the symptoms of the disease is a very sore throat and pain in swallowing. That was one of their main complaints—that and extreme weakness, weakness that you suffer of. It is difficult to imagine lying on a bed and suffering from being weak. Even lifting their head was a big, huge effort.[4]

Rollin agreed:

> They all were very tired. Some say that they had headache, chest pain, back pain. Most of them do not want to talk, they are too exhausted to talk. They do not want to do anything, they just want to die. That is one of the signs of Ebola: people are really very exhausted, the whole time.[5]

Something else the patients had in common was a fixed, upward stare. Their faces were expressionless masks.

Calain continued:

> At the end of the disease the patient does not look, from the outside, as horrible as you can read in some books: they are not 'melting,' they are not full of blood. They are in shock, muscular shock. They are not unconscious, but you would say 'obtunded'—dull, quiet, very tired.[6]

Despite Ebola's reputation, "Very few were hemorrhaging; hemorrhage is not the main symptom," Rollin said. "Less than half of the patients had some kind of hemorrhage."

But, he added, "the ones that bled, died."[7]

# 4

# Diagnosing Ebola Hemorrhagic Fever

**W**hen Ebola hemorrhagic fever reappeared in Kikwit General Hospital in 1995, no one knew at first what it was. Tamfum Muyembe, a virologist from the University of Kinshasa, was called in to assess the situation. He had been at the original Ebola outbreak in Yambuku in 1976, and so was familiar with the disease.

Muyembe arrived in Kikwit on May 1, 1995, learned what was known about the outbreak so far, and correctly deduced that a viral hemorrhagic fever of some sort was to blame. However, the only way to be sure that it was Ebola was to send blood samples to a qualified lab, one with the capability to work safely with the world's most dangerous diseases. Such labs are rare—and there was no such lab in Zaire.

Instead, Muyembe had a military nurse draw blood from fourteen patients on May 4 and 5. Then, he placed the samples in a metal canister, stuffed cotton wadding around the tubes, put the canister in a plastic box, and then filled the box with ice. His plan was to send the samples to the Institute of Tropical Medicine in Antwerp, Belgium. (Zaire had close ties with Belgium; until it claimed its independence in 1960, it was a colony of Belgium known as the Belgian Congo.)

Muyembe gave the samples to Monsignor Nicol, the French deputy bishop, along with a diagram, "Relationship among cases at Kikwit," that showed the probable path the disease had taken from victim to victim, and a letter for Dr. Jean-Pierre Lahaye at the Belgian embassy in Kinshasa.

Monsignor Nicol flew to Kinshasa on May 5. He delivered the samples to Dr. Lahaye, who read Muyembe's letter. The letter directed him to open the box, renew the ice, and then forward the samples to Belgium.

Going through proper channels to get the samples out of Zaire and into Belgium would have taken hours or even days. Because of the urgency, the samples were instead sent with a Zairian woman who made frequent business trips to Belgium. She took them on the plane as carry-on luggage.[1] She delivered them to Dr. Johan van Mullem, who worked at the Brussels headquarters of the Belgian Development Cooperation. It was the weekend and his office was closed, so he took the samples home with him.

The next morning, he called Simon Van Nieuwenhove, a colleague of his, who was in charge of the medical projects funded by the Central Africa Service of their agency and who was familiar with Ebola, having been at both the Yambuku and Sudan outbreaks in 1976. Van Nieuwenhove picked up the samples and drove them to Antwerp to deliver them to Professor Guido van der Groen.

Back in 1976, van der Groen's lab had received the first specimens from Yambuku and had tested them. He had been the first person to see the virus under the electron microscope and had taken the first photograph of it.[2] "This time I could not do anything with them," he said. "I no longer had the proper biosafety lab, I no longer had the diagnostic tools to make a rapid diagnosis, and so I had to send them on the CDC."[3]

He took the samples to his lab, opened the box to make sure the samples were not leaking, and then froze everything. Then, he set about trying to get the samples out of the country. Unfortunately, not only was it the weekend, it was a long weekend: Monday was a holiday, and everything was closed. But, with difficulty, he eventually located some dry ice to pack into the box, found the Federal Express office, and convinced the clerk to accept the box for shipment, "by looking in a convincing way into the charming eyes of the young lady."[4]

The samples finally made it to the Centers for Disease Control and Prevention in Atlanta on Tuesday, May 9, where Tom Ksiazek, laboratory chief of the Special Pathogens Branch, received them. He and Pierre Rollin, chief of the pathogenesis section, put on surgical gowns and gloves and took the box into the Level 3 biosafety lab (see page 43). There, they opened the outer cardboard box. Inside that was a Styrofoam shipper, and inside that, packed in dry ice, was the metal canister which contained, in Ziploc plastic bags, frozen vials of whole blood.

The information on the vials, which indicated what patient the blood was from and when it was drawn, was entered into the computer. Then, Rollin climbed into a "space suit"—a suit that completely encases the wearer in plastic and has its own air supply separate from the air supply in the room—and went through an air lock in the Level 4 biosafety lab, which is completely sealed away from the outside world so that nothing can escape from it.

Rollin first defrosted the samples, then divided them into smaller portions. He set some of these portions to one side,

The biohazard logo, shown here, warns people that there are hazardous products or dangerous biological research in the area.

# What Are Biosafety Levels?

Biosafety levels describe the types of measures in place in a laboratory to prevent the accidental escape of the bacteria or viruses being worked with there.

There are four levels of biosafety:

- **Biosafety Level 1** labs are for working with microorganisms not known to cause disease in healthy human adults. No special protective measures are involved, other than a sink for hand washing.

- **Biosafety Level 2** labs are for working with microorganisms that do cause disease, but can be worked with safely on an open bench, provided there is little risk of splashing or spraying. Splash shields, face protection equipment, gowns and gloves, and closed cabinets are used as required.

- **Biosafety Level 3** labs are for working with microorganisms that could be transmitted through respiration and can cause serious and potentially lethal infections (tuberculosis bacteria is one example). In Biosafety Level 3 labs, all manipulation of samples is done inside a closed, airtight cabinet. Biosafety Level 3 labs usually have controlled access and their own ventilation system to prevent the escape of infectious airborne particles.

- **Biosafety Level 4** labs are for working with dangerous and exotic agents that pose a high individual risk of life-threatening disease, which may be transmitted via the air, and for which there is no available vaccine or therapy (Ebola hemorrhagic fever, for example). In Biosafety Level 4 labs, all workers wear "spacesuits" with an air supply from outside the lab. The lab has its own ventilation system and neither air nor waste materials are released without first being thoroughly decontaminated.

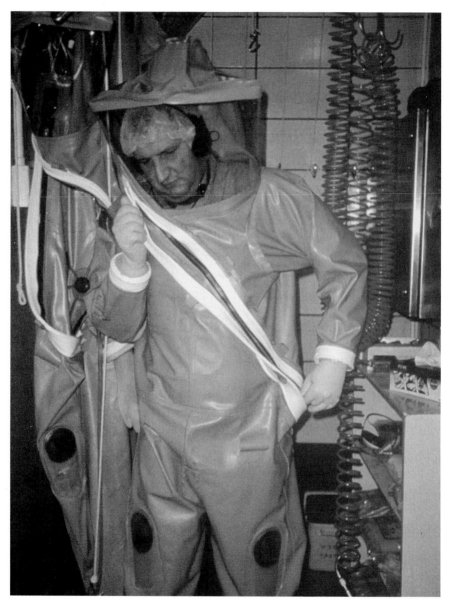

Scientists must put on biosafety suits and face masks before entering Biosafety Level 4 laboratories.

then irradiated the rest with gamma rays to kill any virus they contained, so he could work with the samples outside of the Level 4 lab.

He took the irradiated samples out of the Level 4 lab into a Level 3 lab and handed them over to Mary Lane Martin, a research microbiologist. And it was she, days after the samples were taken and thousands of miles from the site of the outbreak, who finally made the diagnosis: the patients in Kikwit were indeed infected with the Ebola virus.[5]

## No Easy Way to Diagnose

As the previous story shows, there is no easy way to diagnose Ebola hemorrhagic fever. It cannot be done in your average hospital, even a well-stocked Western hospital, and certainly not in a poorly stocked hospital in Africa. Blood samples from living patients or tissue samples from dead ones must be sent to a high-biosafety laboratory, which often means a delay of days, during which time the virus continues to spread.

Nevertheless, the tests have to be done in order to confirm that the disease is Ebola. As was pointed out in the last chapter, Ebola looks very much like many other tropical diseases during its early stages.

To test the samples from Kikwit, Mary Lane Martin first took a prepared plastic plate, then placed measured amounts of the samples into the ninety-six wells that dimpled the plate. Then she conducted what is known as an ELISA (enzyme-linked immunosorbent assay) test. ELISA tests are the standard procedure for identifying unknown viruses. A sample of the unknown virus is added to an enzyme that reacts chemically to only one specific virus. In the presence of the right virus, the enzyme turns a specific color (green, in the case of the test for Ebola virus). Once one of the enzymes turns color, it is clear what virus has been identified.

The actual procedure is a bit more complicated. Various reagents have to be deposited in the right order, washed off again, then mixed with something else, and sometimes incubated. It took Martin about three hours to actually get the samples to the point where she could add the last reagent—the one that would turn green if Ebola virus was present.

"I could see immediately when I added the last reagent that it was going to be positive," Martin said. "It started the color change almost immediately. I knew right away that they were going to be positive."[6]

## Virus Isolation

The ELISA test is not the only way to diagnose Ebola hemorrhagic fever. Another method is to grow any viruses that are in a blood sample in a culture.

This has its own problems, as another story shows.

On November 6, 1996, nurse Marilyn Lahana was admitted to the Sandton Clinic, north of Johannesburg, South Africa, complaining of a severe headache, diarrhea, loss of appetite, and a high temperature. She was tested for malaria, meningitis, typhoid, and many other diseases, but did not have any of them.

However, Dr. Reeve Jobson, who was caring for Lahana, knew that there had recently been an outbreak of Congo fever, a less-virulent type of viral hemorrhagic fever than Ebola, and suspected that might be Lahana's illness. On November 9, he sent ten milliliters of Lahana's blood to South Africa's National Institute for Virology, asking them to test for viral hemorrhagic fevers.

The first test was to check her blood for antibodies to various viral hemorrhagic fevers. Nothing turned up, so Jobson decided that he had been wrong and Lahana probably did not have a viral hemorrhagic fever.

However, this test, which can be carried out fairly quickly, only turns up positive results later in the course of the disease or in the blood of patients who recover. For that reason, the laboratory also began to grow culture of the viruses found in Lahana's blood. Once enough viruses have been grown, they can be identified.

Unfortunately, that takes a week, and in the meantime, Lahana got weaker and weaker. Her stomach was swollen and her liver inflamed, and so Jobson decided she needed surgery. The surgery, which was performed on November 15, revealed that she had been bleeding internally, a sign of viral hemorrhagic fever, but in the absence of confirmation from the lab, they still thought she might have something else, such as typhoid.

Then, later that same day, the laboratory reported that there was a 50 percent chance, based on the viral culture, that Lahana had Ebola. By midnight that had increased to 80 percent, and the next day the lab was certain.

Further research revealed that Lahana had contracted the disease while assisting in an operation on a doctor from Gabon, which was suffering an Ebola outbreak at the time. The doctor recovered, and no one ever suspected he had had Ebola—until Lahana became ill.[7]

The fact she had Ebola meant the operation carried out on her by Jobson was enormously risky—and the fact that the diagnosis by viral culture took so long meant the surgical team carrying out that operation did not even know the risk they faced.

And despite extensive treatment in a modern hospital, Lahana died.

## Polymerase Chain Reaction

The other method of diagnosing Ebola hemorrhagic fever is polymerase chain reaction (PCR). In PCR, a portion of the virus's genetic material is replicated a million times or more using substances known as primers. These primers work only on specific viruses, so if the viral genetic material is successfully replicated, that is proof that the virus being tested is what you think it is.

Again, however, PCR can only be carried out in specialized labs. It is also a very expensive test.[8]

No matter which method is used, Ebola remains tremendously difficult to diagnose quickly and with certainty. Only laboratories with the necessary high level of biosafety can handle the samples, and the materials used in the tests are not commercially available, which further limits the number of labs equipped to do the tests.

Because of this, the safest approach for hospitals in the areas where Ebola outbreaks occur is to always consider Ebola a possibility when a patient shows up with nonspecific early symptoms such as red, itchy eyes and a skin rash, and to take the necessary precautions sooner rather than later.[9]

# 5

# Treatment of Ebola Hemorrhagic Fever

In 1979, Joe McCormick and Roy Baron of the Centers for Disease Control and Prevention Special Pathogens Branch flew to southern Sudan to investigate a new outbreak of Ebola hemorrhagic fever in the town of Nzara.

They collected blood samples from patients suffering and dying from the disease. The samples were sent back to the Centers for Disease Control and Prevention in Atlanta.

Then, they set up a makeshift laboratory and began routinely testing the blood of patients brought in on carts and stretchers by their families. As McCormick began drawing blood from one very ill and frail elderly woman, she jerked. The needle slipped, and he saw with horror a bright red drop of blood ooze out of the thumb of his glove. He had stuck himself with the needle.

"I knew, more than most people," said McCormick, "that when you get stuck by a potentially contaminated needle in the midst of a deadly epidemic, the odds for survival are not very good."

After some thought, he decided to wait and see if he developed symptoms rather than leave, which would have shut down the investigation. He knew that if he had been infected, he would begin to experience the early symptoms of severe headache, fever, and body pains within three to ten days.

The two CDC doctors had brought with them several units of plasma collected three years before from patients who had survived a previous Ebola outbreak in Nzara. McCormick had Baron set up an intravenous line and give him some of the old plasma.

While he waited to see if he would fall ill, McCormick continued his work and kept particularly close watch on the old woman he had been drawing blood from when the accident occurred. One evening he was surprised to see her sitting up and talking to relatives, her fever gone. He knew that if she had recovered from Ebola, as about half those who contract Ebola-Sudan do, her blood would carry antibodies. If she had those antibodies, it would prove that she had, indeed, had Ebola—and that he had been exposed to it.

He ran the necessary tests. Her blood was free of antibodies. He had never been exposed.[1]

But both his fear at the prospect and the fatalism with which he greeted it point to one inescapable fact: There is no treatment for Ebola hemorrhagic fever.

## Treating the Symptoms

As with other diseases for which there is no standard treatment, patients who are suffering from Ebola receive "supportive therapy." This is therapy designed to keep their bodies functioning in the hope that their immune systems will rally to fight off the infection on their own.

Basically, supportive therapy consists of balancing the patients' fluids and electrolytes, making sure they are getting enough oxygen, trying to keep up their blood pressure, and treating them for any complicating, secondary infections.[2] This at least maximizes the chances of patients recovering on their own. Unfortunately, this kind of supportive therapy requires a modern hospital, and most Ebola outbreaks occur where medical facilities are primitive. As a result, most of the focus is on stopping the chain of transmission rather than treating patients who already have the disease.

For instance, in Kikwit, infusions to keep up fluid levels were rarely given to patients in the early stages of the outbreak, even when they were severely dehydrated, and up to 80 percent of those early patients died. The fatality rate dropped once health-care workers had been trained in supportive therapy and there were fewer patients in hospitals.[3]

The lack of a standard treatment does not mean that a number of nonstandard treatments, such as McCormick's choice to be injected with plasma from survivors of the 1976 outbreak, have not been tried. Unfortunately, none of them have been thoroughly tested.

During the large outbreak in Kikwit, Zaire, in 1995, eight patients were similarly given blood from patients who had been infected with Ebola but survived. Seven of the eight patients who received the blood also survived, but because the study size was so small and because those who were chosen to receive the blood were already the ones who seemed most likely to recover, no one is certain if the treatment really worked.[4] Other attempts to treat Ebola patients with blood transfusions from recovered patients have been far less successful. This treatment is also difficult to use because both the donor and recipient must have the same blood type, and there is the risk of transferring other viruses, such as HIV, the virus that causes AIDS.[5]

Other attempts at treatment have included intravenous therapy with heparin to prevent hemorrhaging, and, once hemorrhaging begins, therapy with platelets and clotting factors, which help the blood to clot. This, too, often proves ineffective.[6]

At least one type of treatment that may have been effective—although, again, no one can be certain—happened by accident.

The doctor from Gabon, who unwittingly brought Ebola to South Africa and infected the nurse Lahana, was treated with steroids because the doctors in South Africa thought he might have an autoimmune disease (a disease where the body's own immune system attacks it; rheumatoid arthritis is one example). He seemed to respond very well and recovered completely.[7] However, no one knows if he recovered because of the steroids or if he was recovering anyway.

Although there are no proven treatments for Ebola, research is pointing the way for better treatments in the future, including a possible vaccine. For now, in the absence of treatment options, the most important goal of doctors faced with an Ebola outbreak is to prevent the outbreak from spreading further.

# 6

# Social Implications of Ebola Hemorrhagic Fever

I n early 1996, a distant relative who lived in the rain forest visited the home of Bernard Massika, chieftain of the village of Epassendje, Gabon. Shortly after that, one by one, Massika's family began to die.

The younger of his two wives lapsed into a feverish coma, and her skin turned a deathly blue-black. His eight-year-old daughter began vomiting and coughing up blood.

A month later, ten members of Massika's family—including all nine of his children—were dead.

Massika was replaced as chieftain by his younger brother, whose household was not affected, because villagers believed Massika's family was cursed.

Massika and other relatives were forced to flee from Epassendje. They ended up in the town of Makokou. Massika's remaining wife, Pauline, who nearly died of the disease, no longer spoke to her family and refused to shake hands with strangers.

Massika was told that the cause of his family's death was something called Ebola hemorrhagic fever, but he did not believe it. "This was not a disease," he said. "We were attacked by powerful spirits of darkness." Other Gabonese felt the same way, blaming Ebola's nasty symptoms on witches, ghouls, and vampires.[1]

The same supernatural explanations surfaced in the outbreak in Uganda in 2000. Justin Okot, a neighbor of Esther Owete, one of the first to die in that outbreak, said, "We did not understand that someone could die that quickly. We began calling this thing '*gemo*,' which in Luo (the local language) is a type of ghost or evil spirit. No one knows about it, but it comes and takes you in the night."[2]

It was the only explanation that made sense to them. The speed with which people died and the horrible way in which they died was too terrifying to put down to mere disease. Surely, they must be victims of black magic. As Massika wondered, "How can I believe all of this was just an accident? My enemies are working against me."[3]

Those who do not believe in black magic may put the disease down to punishment from God. Serafin Emputu, who lived in Kikwit near a house where seven people died, said they died because they did not pray. "I know that the persons who believed firmly in God, believed in Jesus Christ, would not be infected, and my neighbors, they did not pray at all," she said.[4]

# Terrifying and Disruptive

An outbreak of Ebola has a way of terrifying and disrupting society far out of proportion to the actual number of deaths the disease causes, due to the ways in which it is typically spread: through unsafe practices in hospitals, and through close contact with family members who have already contracted the disease.

Because the disease has often spread through, and been spread by, hospitals, one of the effects of an outbreak is distrust in doctors and hospitals. This has far-ranging consequences, as people may be less likely to go to the hospital in the future for treatment for diseases that can be cured or controlled.

Ali Kahn, epidemiology chief of the Special Pathogens Branch of the Centers for Disease Control and Prevention at the time of the Kikwit outbreak, remembered all sorts of resistance to going to the hospital. "There was a guy who was found hiding in a barrel at his second wife's house, people hiding other cases. For a lot of people, the outbreak was associated with the hospital, and the hospital was where you went to die."[5]

In the months following the end of the outbreak in Kikwit, Kikwit General Hospital was almost empty. Before the epidemic, it was often so full that in many wards two people shared every bed.

Madar Minioko, a lay pastor in Kikwit, claimed it was because health workers were no longer helping the sick. He said that he went to the hospital with a sick friend who had a high fever from malaria, but the nurse refused to take his blood or give him an injection, instead asking the friend's wife to do it. Minioko said it was not an unusual story, and it made him so mad he would rather die at home than go to a clinic or hospital.[6]

The workers at the hospital denied anyone was being refused treatment, but admitted they were afraid. "Before the epidemic, even when we did not have the protective material, we worked, and we were touching patients, and we had confidence and trust in our patients," said Rosalee Mumpia, chief surgical nurse. "But, since this epidemic, we have seen many of our colleagues have died. That is why we are afraid."[7]

That fear is justified, since so many health care workers have died in the various Ebola outbreaks. And the loss of nurses and doctors is another blow the disease deals to the communities in which it surfaces.

One of the victims of the Ugandan outbreak, for instance, was Dr. Matthew Lukwiya, the medical superintendent of Lacor Hospital in Gulu. Summoned back to Gulu from Kampala when patients began dying, he was the one who recognized that the mysterious disease might be Ebola and, after confirmation from South African laboratories, raised the global alarm.

By using modern nursing techniques and educating the local population about how the disease was spread, he managed to contain the outbreak to the immediate region. It is safe to say that without his early efforts, the outbreak would have been much worse. Unfortunately, at some point he must have failed to take the proper precautions himself. He fell ill on November 30 and died on December 5.[8] "Ebola virus is not very forgiving," said Dr. Ray Arthur, the World Health Organization Ebola coordinator in Gulu. "One little mistake is enough to infect an individual."[9]

Lukwiya was the fourteenth medical worker to die in the Ugandan outbreak.

## Traditions Suffer

Traditional lifestyles are another victim of Ebola. In the cultures in which it has surfaced, family members care for people who are sick, and when someone dies, family members prepare the body for burial. Unfortunately, because Ebola hemorrhagic fever is transmitted by contact with bodily fluids, both of these are high-risk activities. So are other seemingly ordinary activities such as embracing friends and family and sharing eating utensils.

One of the things Dr. Lukwiya did to contain the Ugandan outbreak was to convince radio broadcasters to tell Gulu residents what they could do to protect themselves: avoiding shaking hands, sharing cups or plates, and particularly, taking part in the traditional ritualistic, communal washing of the dead.[10]

When Dr. Lukwiya himself was buried, his body was sealed within a plastic shroud; his pallbearers wore latex gloves and surgical masks; and his friends and family were not allowed to touch the body.[11]

The necessity of abandoning traditional funeral practices is particularly hard on communities suffering from so much unexpected, horrible death.

In the interest of safety, residents were told to forego their traditional burial rituals. Instead, the Red Cross and other workers sterilized the body bags of Ebola victims and buried them to ensure that the virus did not spread any further.

As Madar Minioko put it, in Kikwit, "Before, it was our custom to never leave a corpse alone. When someone died, all the family and the clan were always around the body, touching it and crying over it. We washed the body, changed its clothes, arranged it in a comfortable coffin, and only then did we feel we had respected and properly buried the relative."[12]

That stopped during the outbreak. Teams of Red Cross workers dressed in helmets, boots, gloves, and goggles simply gathered the bodies, zipped them into body bags, and buried them without ceremony.

Paranoia strikes deep at the heart of a community stricken by Ebola. Beatric Sona's husband became sick after helping the family of an ill neighbor during the Kikwit outbreak. But when her husband died, no one came to help her. According to Sona:

> It was very painful, of course. We had been living with people and suddenly they flee. We could not even go to our neighbors to ask for some fire to get burning charcoal. We could not send children to take things to our neighbors. It was impossible to have any contact with them.[13]

## Survivors Shunned

Surviving the disease does not necessarily make things any easier.

James Akena, a forty-year-old farmer, was one of those who contracted Ebola and survived during the outbreak in Gulu, Uganda. When he was released from the hospital, he was given a letter certifying that he could "go home and is no longer dangerous to his community."

"When I was discharged a nurse took me home," he said. "We found my house and all my belongings burned, and my neighbors chased us away."[14]

With no home and no money, Akena spent several days without food in an outdoor bus station until health workers who were following up on his case discovered him. Eventually, the government resettled him into another part of Uganda.

Lucy Akidi had a similar story. "When my in-laws heard that I was discharged, they sent someone to tell me to go straight to my parents' compound and never return to theirs. But my husband resisted and said I would return, even if it meant living in isolation. My in-laws fled when we arrived."[15]

These kinds of fears are common wherever Ebola surfaces, and make it imperative that medical workers explain as clearly as possible how the disease is transmitted and that survivors are not infectious.

## Whole World Paranoid

But paranoia is not confined to the places directly affected by Ebola. The whole world, it sometimes seems, is paranoid about Ebola, which makes every outbreak of the disease big news—even though there are diseases that kill far more people that do not make the news at all. For example, between October 14, 2000 and January 25, 2001, 427 Ebola cases were reported in Uganda, with 173 deaths. During the same time, there were more than 1,900 media references to the disease in the Nexis online database. That is eleven media mentions per fatality.[16]

But that is not surprising, because journalists from around the world rush to the site of any new outbreak.

The outbreak does not even have to be real. In February of 2001, Colette Matshimoseka fell ill in Hamilton, Ontario, after arriving on a visit from the Democratic Republic of the Congo. She was admitted to the hospital with a high fever. Doctors did not know what was wrong with her, but because she had come from the Congo, they isolated her and sent samples of her blood to the Centers for Disease Control and Prevention and Canada's own Level 4 biosafety laboratory in Winnipeg, Manitoba.

All the major television news networks sent reporters to the hospital, and doctors gave daily news conferences . . . until it was determined that she did not, in fact, have Ebola. Then the news interest vanished.[17]

To put it in perspective, Ebola hemorrhagic fever has killed fewer than 1,000 people since the virus first surfaced in 1976. Tuberculosis, on the other hand, kills at least two million people around the world every year—or five times more people every day than Ebola has killed in more than a quarter of a century. In any large city, pneumonia will kill as many people in an average year as Ebola has ever killed.[18] Malaria kills 700,000 people every year in sub-Saharan Africa. Diarrhea—which people joke about in North America—kills about 900,000.[19]

So why does Ebola hemorrhagic fever fascinate and frighten people so much?

"It has to do with public perception," says Dr. Jay Keystone, staff physician at Toronto General Hospital's Centre for Travel and Tropical Medicine. "Suddenly this is the plague. Ebola is in our face, through the media. That is why we're so afraid of it."[20]

## The Hot Zone

Public perception of Ebola as a particularly frightening disease probably began with a story by Richard Preston called "Crisis in the Hot Zone" that was published in *The New Yorker* on October 26, 1992. That eventually became the book *The Hot Zone*, which was a best-seller.

Preston's *The Hot Zone* told the story of the outbreak of Ebola-Reston among monkeys in Reston, Virginia, and included the story of Ebola outbreaks in Africa. Because it appears that Ebola-Reston may have been transmitted via airborne particles like the common cold, Preston suggested that the more deadly forms of Ebola could mutate to do the same thing. That would set the stage for a hard-to-control epidemic that could threaten the whole world.

*The Hot Zone* inspired *Outbreak*, a movie starring Dustin Hoffman, in which a fictional Ebola-like disease threatened the United States. Then there was a TV movie, *Virus*, starring Ebola itself.

*The Coming Plague*, a Pulitzer Prize–winning book by Laurie Garrett, also suggested that an apocalyptic outbreak of Ebola or some other, currently unknown, disease could be just around the corner.

Newspapers and magazines have also contributed somewhat sensationalized articles and stories. In December 2000, *Business Week* ran a story called, "Ebola Could Soon Be the West's Problem, Too," that opened with the line, "There is a crisis brewing in the world that we ignore at our peril. The Ebola virus is back, and it is spreading."

These fears are based on certain common misconceptions about Ebola (see page 66), including that it is highly contagious, that it is the deadliest disease known to man, and that it could cause an enormous epidemic if it ever reached North America.

In fact, according to Don Low, one of Canada's leading microbiologists, the risk of a North American Ebola epidemic is effectively zero.[21]

Dr. C. J. Peters, chief of the Special Pathogens Branch at the Centers for Disease Control and Prevention, puts it this way: "It is possible that someone with Ebola might leave a remote area where the disease is occurring and might even get sick here." But, "because our socioeconomic level allows high standards in hospitals, there would be a few cases but they would be controllable under our circumstances."

## A Useful Metaphor

One reason Ebola gets so much media attention despite the fact that it is a relative pipsqueak of a killer, as far as infectious diseases go, is that it is a useful metaphor for the idea that our encroachment into areas of the world where people have not lived before holds the potential to unleash another terrifying epidemic like AIDS.

# Five Widely Believed Myths About Ebola

Here are five myths about Ebola that many people believe:

1. **Ebola is highly infectious**. It is not. "You have to work hard to get it from a person," Ralph Henderson, assistant director general of the World Health Organization, said at the time of the Kikwit outbreak. The disease is transmitted through contact with bodily fluids, so latex gloves, face masks, and other simple barriers are enough to prevent infection.

2. **Ebola can easily travel through the air to infect people**. Ebola cannot travel through the air unless airborne droplets—created when an infected person coughs or sneezes—are inhaled or brought into contact with other mucous membranes.

3. **The virus could rapidly mutate into a form that could be transmitted through the air**. Although Ebola is a type of virus that tends to mutate rapidly, such a change is unlikely. According to Mary Wilson, an infectious disease specialist and professor at Harvard, "Even if there are mutations and changes in the virus, it does not mean it will change its basic mechanism of attaching to a cell."

4. **Ebola could come to the United States via an infected passenger on an international flight**. That, too, is highly unlikely. "The chance of someone getting on an airplane with this disease is just vanishingly small," said Henderson. The disease is not infectious during the incubation period, which is the only time someone suffering from it would be in any condition to travel. By the time they are bleeding, they are too sick to get on an airplane.

5. **Ebola is the most dangerous disease ever encountered.** Although it is certainly a nasty disease, it is much more easily contained than viruses such as HIV, which people can carry around with them for years, infecting others, before they show symptoms. Ebola kills so quickly, and is infectious for such a short period of the disease's course, that it does not have much chance to spread.[22]

In *The Hot Zone*, Richard Preston writes,

> In a sense, the earth is mounting an immune response against
> the human species. . . . Perhaps the biosphere does not
> 'like' the idea of five billion humans. . . . The earth's immune
> system, so to speak, has recognized the presence of the human
> species and is starting to kick in. The earth is attempting to
> rid itself of an infection by the human parasite."[23]

Statements like that account for a lot of Western "Ebola
fever," but those who have firsthand experience with
Ebola make it clear that if Earth is trying rid itself of
humans, it is not going to manage it with Ebola hemorrhagic fever.

Margaretha Isaäcson, a South African physician who dealt
with Ebola at Ngaliema Hospital in Kinshasa, Zaire, during
the original 1976 outbreak, puts it this way:

> Ebola is of absolutely no danger to the world at large. It is a
> dangerous virus, but it is relatively rare and quite easily
> contained. The virus needs the right conditions to multiply,
> whatever the virus is, be it Ebola or plague. It is not enough
> to just have the accident. The virus must first find itself in a
> favorable environment before it can affect anyone. The
> media is scaring the world out of its wits, and movies like
> *Outbreak* are doing people a great disservice."[24]

Yet even if the media attention given to Ebola is unwar-
ranted, it has had its good side. "It has contributed to piling
pressure on decision-makers," says Guido van der Groen of
the Antwerp Institute of Tropical Medicine. "It helped develop
initiatives at the highest level between Europe and the United

States to try and make an inventory of infectious diseases and help coordinate surveillance."[25] That means that if another new disease appears, as Preston and others fear, doctors and scientists should find out about it more quickly and have procedures in place to deal with it.

But Ebola's overall affect on society, van der Groen said, is:

> . . . peanuts compared with other problems. If they call Ebola a killer what would you say to a virus like HIV or Hepatitis B? I call Ebola a macho virus because it immediately wants to prove it is there . . . people know within two or three days it entered their body and they can tell doctors, relatives he or she is ill. And if suddenly in a village ten or fifteen people have it they are isolated.[26]

Yet, as the accounts earlier in this chapter from places where Ebola hemorrhagic fever has cropped up show, the disease remains a serious threat to society on a local—if not a global—level. And that, says van der Groen, will continue for as long as the infrastructure in many developing countries remains poor.[27]

# 7

# Preventing Ebola Hemorrhagic Fever

In 1976, when Ebola hemorrhagic fever surfaced for the first time in Yambuku, one of the nuns who was infected, Sister M. E., flew to Kinshasa with another nun who acted as her nurse, Sister E. R., and a priest. All three were admitted to Ngaliema Hospital, where they were attended by Margaretha Isaäcson, a South African physician, and a Zairian nurse named Mayinga.

Later, Isaäcson explained how she dealt with her three new patients. "From the moment of the arrival of the two nuns and the priest . . . on twenty-five September 1976, some precautionary measures were taken to prevent spread of the infection," she said. "Barrier nursing was introduced at the start, and cotton gowns and cotton masks were worn when attending the patient. These were later replaced by disposable gowns and masks, but as supplies were inadequate, the gowns and the disposable plastic overshoes were hung up outside the door of the patient's room for reuse." Isaäcson also noted that Sister E. R. did not wear protective clothing when attending Sister M. E.[1]

Sister M. E. died on September 30. Eight days later, Sister E. R. fell ill; she died on October 14. In the entire hospital, one of the biggest in the city, the only other person who acquired the disease was nurse Mayinga, who had been in contact with the first nun for several days prior to her death. Researchers assume that at some point she failed to follow proper safety procedures.

Nobody else got the disease, even though Mayinga, after she developed symptoms, spent several hours in a crowded emergency room at Mama Yemo Hospital (also in Kinshasa), where she shared a bottle of soda with a young boy and shared food off the plate of a fourteen-year-old girl.

## Basic Principles of Prevention

Isaäcson concluded that "it appears that the observation of the basic principles of aseptic technique or barrier nursing are probably effective in breaking the chain of infection," that "airborne dissemination of the virus did not play a major role, if any, in the transmission of the disease," and "the Ebola virus is not highly infectious and requires very close contact, primarily with blood or secretions, for its transmission."[2]

A quarter of a century later, those conclusions remain intact. The spread of Ebola, once an outbreak has occurred, can be halted with fairly simple safety precautions that basically consist of erecting a barrier around the people who are infected, by isolating them and covering those who tend to them with protective clothing.

## Dealing With Suspected Cases Step-By-Step

The Centers for Disease Control and Prevention provides precise guidelines for dealing with patients with suspected hemorrhagic fever—Lassa, Marburg, and Congo-Crimean as well as Ebola.

The first step is to report the suspected case to local and state health departments and to the CDC, which will then make arrangements for samples to be sent to it at once for diagnostic tests.

The CDC says that viral hemorrhagic fever is to be suspected when patients have, within the previous three weeks, either traveled in the specific local area of a country where an outbreak has occurred, had direct contact with blood or other body fluids of a person or animal with a viral hemorrhagic fever, or worked in a laboratory or animal facility that handles hemorrhagic fever viruses. If the person has simply been in a country where viral hemorrhagic fevers sometimes occur, but there has not been a recent outbreak, the infection is more likely to be something more common, such as malaria or typhoid.

While being checked over either in the emergency room at the hospital or by paramedics prior to being taken by ambulance to a hospital, patients are unlikely to be in the highly infective stage of the disease. This means that simple precautions, such as gloves and face shields or surgical masks and eye protection, are sufficient to prevent contact with droplets in the event of coughing or sneezing.

Once the patient reaches the hospital, he or she should be given a private room—one with negative pressure, if possible. (*Negative pressure* means that the air inside the room has a lower pressure than the outside air, so that air from inside the room cannot escape.) That is not because the patient is highly infectious yet, but so that he or she will not need to be moved to a negative-pressure room later in the illness, if it turns out to be a viral hemorrhagic fever.

The CDC recommends that nonessential staff and visitors should be kept out of the room. Nurses and others who enter the room should wear gloves and gowns at a minimum, with the addition of face protection if they will be coming within approximately three feet (one meter) of the patient. Additional barriers may be needed, depending on circumstances. If blood, other body fluids, vomit, or feces are present on the floor, for instance, leg and shoe coverings might be needed, too. Upon leaving the room, all protective clothing should be removed and shoes soiled with body fluids should be cleaned and disinfected. (That can be accomplished by soaking in as simple a concoction as a 1:100 dilution of household bleach for five minutes.)

If the patient has a prominent cough, vomiting, diarrhea, or hemorrhage, protective respirators are recommended for people entering the room. (That is just to be completely safe. The CDC points out that airborne transmission involving humans has never been documented and is considered a possibility only in rare instances from people with advanced stages of the disease.)

One of the greatest hazards facing medical workers is the possibility of accidentally sticking themselves with a contaminated needle or other sharp instrument, so special care has to be taken whenever using such devices. Special care also has

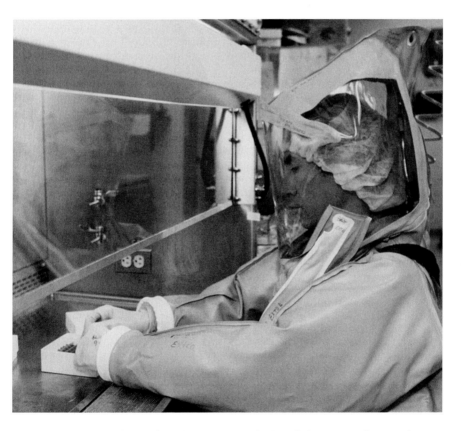

Samples taken from infected patients must be handled in a Biosafety Level 4 laboratory, like this one at the Centers for Disease Control and Prevention in Atlanta, Georgia.

to be taken in packaging samples taken from patients and within the hospital laboratory when tests are being done on those samples. Isolating and cultivating any virus in the samples has to be done in a Level 4 biosafety lab, such as the one at the Centers for Disease Control and Prevention.

Everything used in the room has to be carefully handled and decontaminated; soiled linens, for instance, must be placed in clearly labeled leakproof bags and either washed thoroughly with hot water and bleach, or incinerated. Blood and other fluids, along with urine and feces, should be decontaminated (with a bleach solution, for instance) before going into the hospital's sewage disposal system.

If the patient dies, the body should be handled as little as possible. The corpse should be wrapped in a sealed leakproof material and not embalmed. It should be either cremated or buried promptly in a sealed casket.

If someone is exposed to blood or other fluids from a patient with suspected viral hemorrhagic fever, he or she should immediately wash the affected skin surface with soap and water and apply an antiseptic solution. Any mucous membranes affected should be flushed with lots and lots of water.[3]

After that, all the exposed person can do is wait to see what happens.

## Preventing Ebola Harder Than Controlling It

Preventing the spread of Ebola hemorrhagic fever, then, is not that difficult. Plastic and rubber stops it cold, and ordinary bleach kills it.

But preventing the spread of the disease is not the same as preventing the disease. To do that, you need to either create a vaccine or discover where the disease is hiding in the wild. There is some hope that a vaccine may someday be possible— but we do not have one yet. As for finding the disease in the wild, despite intensive efforts after every outbreak, so far researchers have come up empty.

They know that there has to be a natural reservoir of some kind, because the virus obviously does not live in humans all the time; it kills them too quickly. It does not really do a virus any good to kill people too quickly, because when the virus's host dies, it dies, too.

Somewhere, it must live peaceably inside some other living creature, only occasionally making the jump to humans or monkeys.

"Humans are incidental or accidental victims of this disease," says Mike Ryan, a member of the World Health Organization team that went to Uganda to help deal with the 2000–2001 outbreak of Ebola there. "In previous outbreaks, it was humans dealing with sick chimpanzees in the bush meat industry. We go back and we find one single person who was hunting bush meat and who comes out ill and infects his own family, and you get a chain of transmissions."[4]

That might have explained some previous outbreaks, but not the one in Uganda. Gulu, where the outbreak was centered, is surrounded by scrub brush, not jungle, and the people who live there do not normally eat wild animals.

After each outbreak, scientists have scoured the surrounding countryside, collecting samples of all kinds of plants and animals, looking for one that contains Ebola. Although hundreds of species of animals and plants have been examined, the results have so far been inconclusive. However, there are many theories.

Some scientists believe bats could be the natural host for Ebola. Bats were found in the roof of the Nzara Cotton Factory during the 1976 outbreak there. The first person to get the disease in Nzara, as well as two other early victims, all worked in that factory. So did the first person to get Ebola in the second outbreak in Nzara in 1979.

A study done at the National Institute of Virology in South Africa has shown that Ebola can replicate in fruit bats and some other related species, and emerge in their feces.

However, other animal species also lived in the cotton factory, and Ebola has never been found in bats captured during outbreaks. Also, Ebola kills bats quickly, just like it does humans. That could mean that while bats may be able to pass Ebola on to humans, as chimpanzees can, they are still not the main host of the virus.[5]

A second possibility is that Ebola lives in a plant most of the time. One bit of evidence in favor of this idea is that Ebola outbreaks in the chimpanzee population in the Tai Forest of the Ivory Coast seems to coincide with the flowering of a particular species of plant. However, attempts to inoculate several species of plants with Ebola have so far failed to turn up one in which Ebola can replicate.[6]

Just like in humans, the Ebola virus kills bats quickly.

Other researchers have suggested that perhaps, because Ebola tends to kill mammals, it normally resides in insects, instead. Evidence favoring this notion includes the fact that insects are everywhere, all the time, and one study in the 1970s showed that Marburg virus (which is closely related to Ebola) could replicate in mosquitoes. One patient who contracted Marburg in Zimbabwe also had what appeared to be a horsefly or spider bite.

Studies of insects captured at the sites of Ebola outbreaks have failed to turn up Ebola, and recent attempts to replicate the study showing Marburg could reproduce itself inside mosquitoes have failed. But, again, there are thousands of species of insects, and perhaps the right species (which might only carry Ebola part of the time) has yet to be captured and tested at the right place and the right time.[7]

## The Leafhopper Connection

Another bit of evidence that suggests the possibility of an insect connection comes from Denmark, where Dr. Thorben Lundsgaard, a plant researcher in the Danish Royal Veterinary and Agriculture University, has been studying a virus that attacks grasses used to feed livestock in Europe and North America. He thought the virus might be carried to the grasses by tiny flying insects called leafhoppers, so he grew a batch of them, mashed them up, and started scouring cell samples with an electron microscope for signs of the virus. He did not find it. "But I did find something else," he said. "And it was by chance. I see something and then I go, of course, in more detail. I look, and it looks like a filovirus. And I was very excited, in fact."[8]

The virus he found looks similar—although not identical—to Ebola, which raises the possibility that Ebola could live in similar insects in Africa. Jim LeDuc, head of arbovirus control at the World Health Organization, was part of a search by the U.S. Army in 1981 in northern Zaire for Ebola's source. "Everybody in the villages was raising guinea pigs to eat," he remembered. "And they feed the animals these grasses that are loaded with leafhoppers."[9]

Dr. Elena Ryabchikova of the State Research Center of Virology in Novosibirsk, Russia, found that guinea pigs infected with Ebola seemed resistant at first, but after eight generations, a strain of the virus suddenly showed up that killed them all. That could mean, in nature, that guinea pigs can carry the virus, while rarely becoming sick themselves . . . and perhaps they are first infected by leafhoppers.[10]

## "A Complicated Story"

Dr. Tom Monath of Boston has played a key role in numerous investigations of epidemics and was the one who discovered that another hemorrhagic fever, Lassa, was passed on to humans via inhalation of dust contaminated with the urine of brown rats who carried the virus. He believes the Ebola puzzle is likely to be more complex than that. It might involve insects, such as leafhoppers, eaten by animals that were eaten by people, or passed on by a bite to other animals that were eaten by yet another animal or by people. "I'd be very surprised if this does not turn out to be a complicated story," he says.[11]

And until we know how the story goes, we have no hope of preventing future outbreaks of Ebola. We can only hope to minimize their effects through preventative measures after the first cases appear.

That is small comfort for those whose illness signals to the world that Ebola has raised its ugly head once again.

# 8

# Research and Future Prospects

In the spring of 1995, at about the time of the Ebola outbreak in Kikwit, C. J. Peters, Anthony Sanchez, Pierre Rollin, Tom Ksiazek, and Fred Murphy were working on a paper entitled "Filoviridae: Marburg and Ebola Viruses," intended to summarize everything that was then known about these two hemorrhagic fever viruses.

The paper appeared in the 1996 edition of the journal *Field's Virology.* Rather than summarizing knowledge, however, it mostly summarized lack of knowledge.

"We still do not know how filoviruses are maintained in nature," the authors wrote, and "The mode of entry of Marburg and Ebola viruses into cells remains unknown. . . ."

They wrote that the means by which the viruses caused such devastating symptoms still were not understood. They noted that in fatal infections, patients died with high levels of virus particles in their systems but no sign of an immune response, for reasons unknown. They pointed out that no one knew how and why some people recover and some do not.

"The origin in nature and the natural history of Marburg and Ebola viruses remain a mystery," they wrote.[1]

But in just the past few years, we have found the beginnings of answers to some of these mysteries, in the process creating hope that in the not-too-distant future, we may have drugs that can treat Ebola effectively . . . or even a vaccine that can protect people from contracting it in the first place.

## Genetics Holds the Key

One vital piece of information was already known at the time the paper was written: the precise makeup of the Ebola virus' genes.

Genes are the basic unit of heredity; they contain the information passed on from generation to generation of an organism. The Ebola virus has seven genes.

Each gene, in turn, is made up of many thousands of pairs of "bases," the chemicals that serve as a kind of language in which the information for making new copies of the organism is written. Anthony Sanchez of the Centers for Disease Control and Prevention decoded and published the precise combination of molecular bases that made up six of Ebola's seven genes; a group of Russian scientists decoded the seventh.

The complete list of bases contained in all the genes in an organism is called the genome. The Ebola genome turned out to be very large for a virus, meaning that more information is contained in an Ebola virus than in many other viruses.

To determine what a particular gene does in an organism, you can separate it from the rest of the organism's genes and insert it into a cell culture. Since genes tell cells what substances to synthesize, you can sometimes tell what a particular gene does by figuring out what the cells inoculated with the separated gene are synthesizing that they would not normally.

One thing Sanchez found out in his study of Ebola's genes was that one gene did something "very bizarre." Whereas normally one gene results in only one output from a cell, one of Ebola's genes resulted in the creation of two substances: One was the outer surface of the virus, a spiky coat that attaches to molecules on the surfaces of cells and allows the virus to gain entry to it. The other substance, however, was a liquid that did not become part of the virus at all, but instead simply floated away.[2]

No one was sure what purpose that substance, called a glycoprotein, served; however, a comparison of the gene that produces the glycoprotein with other viral genetic codes in a database called GenBank revealed that one small region of the glycoprotein gene was very similar to sections of one of the genes of cancer-causing retroviruses that had been shown to work to weaken the action of the body's immune system. That raised the possibility that Ebola's glycoprotein gene helped explain the fact that Ebola victims seemed to mount no effective immune system response to infection with the virus.[3]

Then, in July 2000, Dr. Gary Nabel of the National Institutes of Health's Vaccine Research Center and his team from the NIH and the Centers for Disease Control and Prevention said they had discovered that the glycoprotein attacks the cells that line blood vessels, called endothelial cells, making them leak and possibly causing much of the devastating hemorrhaging characteristic of the disease.[4]

Nabel's team genetically engineered cultured human endothelial cells so that they produced the Ebola glycoprotein, and found that within twenty-four hours, the cells could no longer stick to one another. The cells all died within a few days.

When the gene coding for glycoprotein was introduced directly into blood vessels surgically removed from pigs or humans, the vessels suffered massive losses of endothelial cells within two days. They became leaky, letting fluids through much more easily.[5]

That holds out hope for drugs that might be able to fight Ebola's effects, Nabel said. "We have been able to define the major Ebola virus gene that kills cells, and have provided a molecular target for potential new antiviral drugs and vaccines."[6]

Nabel's team also discovered that the Ebola-Reston version of Ebola does not damage blood vessels in the same way, which could explain why it is not fatal to humans.

The finding that the glycoprotein attacked endothelial cells does not mean that it does not also suppress the immune system, Nabel noted. "We find it binds to inflammatory cells—it may blunt the inflammatory response to infection."[7]

Not all scientists agree that glycoprotein's attack on endothelial cells is central to the damage caused by Ebola. They note that Ebola and Marburg victims do not have the buildup of fluids in the lungs and the swelling of the head and neck that is usually connected with leaky blood vessels. Also, monkeys infected with Ebola do not show much endothelial cell damage until the end stages of the disease, when the symptoms have been severe for several days. As with most things connected with Ebola, more research is needed.[8]

Another way Ebola keeps the body's immune system in check so it can replicate was discovered just a few months later. In October 2000, when the outbreak in Uganda was in full swing, a team of German and American researchers from Philipps Universtat in Marburg, Germany, and Mount Sinai School of Medicine in New York published a paper in the *Proceedings of the National Academy of Sciences* announcing that they had found a protein, called VP35, that Ebola uses to disable the production of interferon. Interferon is a compound produced by the immune system to kill virus-infected cells before they can spew more viruses into the system.

Those who fight off Ebola successfully may have a stronger immune system that is able to fight off the effects of this protein, the researchers said. They noted that at least one case has been reported of a person who was infected with Ebola but never developed symptoms.[9]

As with the discovery of the function of the glycoprotein, the discovery of VP35 held out hope for more effective drugs in the future.

# A Vaccine?

Hot on the heels of those discoveries came even more exciting news: the possible development of a vaccine.

Again, Dr. Gary Nabel was at the forefront, reporting in November 2000, in the science journal *Nature*, that four vaccinated macaque monkeys survived an injection of Ebola-Zaire, while unvaccinated control animals died within four to seven days.

The vaccinated animals mounted an efficient immune response to the virus and cleared it out of their systems within two weeks. Six months later, they were still healthy.

The vaccine also protected them against Ebola-Ivory Coast and Ebola-Sudan, the other two strains of Ebola that cause disease in humans.[10]

That was not the first vaccine for Ebola; back in 1997, Nabel and colleagues reported that guinea pigs injected with genes from the Ebola virus gained protection against infection from it. In those tests, one group of guinea pigs was vaccinated, then injected with Ebola virus within two months. Fifteen of sixteen vaccinated guinea pigs survived. Six animals that had not been vaccinated were also injected with Ebola; all died.[11]

However, it is a long leap from vaccines that protect guinea pigs to vaccines that protect humans; and while it is a shorter leap from monkeys to humans, there is still no guarantee that an effective human version of the vaccine can be produced.

Vaccines are sometimes created from viruses that have either been killed or weakened so they no longer cause disease,

Some vaccines have been shown to protect against the Ebola virus in guinea pigs.

but such a virus would be unlikely to be accepted in the case of a disease such as Ebola. Instead, Nabel and his colleagues initially followed the same procedure used to create a vaccine in guinea pigs. They created a vaccine from one protein found in the Ebola virus. However, that did not generate enough of an immune response in the monkeys to protect them.

To "rev up" the monkeys' immune systems even more, Nabel and his colleagues gave them a second shot consisting of a weakened cold virus that had been genetically engineered to contain a protein from Ebola-Zaire. The two shots together did the trick.[12]

Peter Jahrling of the U.S. Army Medical Research Institute of Infectious Disease in Fort Detrick, Frederick, Maryland, has also worked with Ebola vaccines in rodents. "While this clearly is a significant step forward, these experiments need to be repeated with a higher challenge dose," he said.

The monkeys in Nabel's study were infected with approximately 100 to 200 virus particles; infected people harbor 10,000 times that number of virus particles in their blood.[13]

Giving the monkeys higher doses, Jahrling said, would indicate whether the vaccine could "protect medical staff caring for patients with Ebola in Africa—they are in contact with infected blood containing extremely high viral doses."[14]

At the time this book was being written, monkey-based studies of the vaccine were continuing, while Dr. Nabel was working with the Food and Drug Administration to begin testing the safety of the vaccine in humans.

"It is important that we recognize that to develop a vaccine against Ebola, or AIDS or even cancer, we learn a lot by animal models, but it is studies in humans that tell us if it is working," he said.[15]

If an effective vaccine can be developed, it would probably be offered first to family members and contacts of those infected in any new outbreak, as well as to health-care professionals. Field workers and laboratory researchers could be offered the vaccine as well. Mass vaccination probably would not occur because of the lack of funding and the difficulty of reaching communities in remote regions of Africa.[16]

Scientists are optimistic. Writing in the November 30, 2000, issue of *Nature*, Dennis R. Burton and Paul W. H. I. Parren of the Departments of Immunology and Molecular Biology at The Scripps Research Institute in La Jolla, California, put it this way:

> There is still some way to go before a human vaccine is available, but this is a step in the right direction . . . it seems hopeful that human vaccination against filoviruses will be achieved.[17]

That will not put an end to outbreaks of Ebola hemorrhagic fever; but maybe, just maybe, it will lessen the fear, sometimes rational, sometimes irrational, caused by this fascinating but terrifying disease.

# Q & A

**Q.** What is Ebola hemorrhagic fever?

**A.** Ebola hemorrhagic fever is a severe, often fatal, disease that affects humans and nonhuman primates (monkeys and chimpanzees). It is caused by infection with the Ebola virus, which was named after a river in the Democratic Republic of the Congo in Africa, near the place where Ebola hemorrhagic fever first surfaced in 1976.

**Q.** Is there more than one kind of Ebola?

**A.** Yes. In fact, there are four different strains that we know of: Ebola-Zaire, Ebola-Sudan, Ebola-Ivory Coast, and Ebola-Reston. The first three all cause disease in humans; Ebola-Reston only affects monkeys.

**Q.** Where is Ebola found in nature?

**A.** We do not know for certain. However, researchers believe it normally lives in an animal native to Africa and only occasionally makes the jump from its host animal to humans, monkeys, and chimpanzees.

**Q.** Where do cases of Ebola hemorrhagic fever occur?

**A.** Confirmed cases of Ebola hemorrhagic fever have been reported in the Democratic Republic of the Congo, Gabon, Sudan, the Ivory Coast, and Uganda. One person whose blood indicated he had been infected, but who did not become sick, was reported in Liberia, and a laboratory worker in England became ill after an accidental needle-stick. No case of the disease in humans has ever been reported in the United States. Ebola-Reston has caused illness and death in monkeys imported into American research facilities from the Philippines.

**Q.** How is Ebola virus spread?

**A.** The first person in an outbreak presumably catches the virus from an animal. After that, the disease spreads primarily through direct contact with the blood and other bodily fluids of an infected person. People can also be exposed to Ebola through contact with contaminated objects, such as needles. In many outbreaks, the disease is spread within hospitals, because in many African hospitals masks, gowns, and gloves are not routinely worn and needles and syringes may be reused.

**Q.** Can Ebola virus be spread through the air?

**A.** Although under research conditions Ebola has shown the ability to spread through airborne particles, there has never been a documented case of a human being infected in this manner in a real-world setting, such as a household or hospital. However, Ebola-Reston may have been passed from monkey to monkey through the air of the research facilities in which it has surfaced.

**Q.** Does Ebola hemorrhagic fever cause people's internal organs to "melt" or rot away?

**A.** No. However, internal bleeding can lead to vomiting large amounts of blood, which may give that impression.

**Q.** Can Ebola hemorrhagic fever be cured?

**A.** No. There is no treatment for the disease at this time. However, in the recent outbreak in Uganda, making sure that patients received plenty of fluids intravenously to replace those lost due to the bleeding caused by Ebola seems to have reduced the death rate.

**Q.** Is Ebola hemorrhagic fever always fatal?

**A.** No. In the outbreaks to date, Ebola-Zaire has been the most deadly, killing up to 88 percent of its victims; Ebola-Sudan kills about half of those who contract it. Those who survive take several weeks to recover.

**Q.** Could someone with Ebola getting on an airplane and flying to the United States cause a major epidemic here?

**A.** No. First, it is unlikely anyone in the final stages of the disease, when it is most contagious, would be well enough to travel. If someone in the earlier stages of the disease were to travel here and then begin exhibiting symptoms, the outbreak would be limited to very few cases. That is because transmission of Ebola can be easily prevented by standard hospital preventative measures.

**Q.** Is Ebola the most dangerous disease ever discovered?

**A.** No. Nasty though it is, it is much more easily contained than viruses such as HIV (which causes AIDS), because people can carry HIV around in their bloodstream for years, potentially infecting other people, before they show any symptoms. Because Ebola kills people so quickly, and they are only highly infectious for a short period of their illness, outbreaks are easily contained.

# Ebola Virus Timeline

**430–426 B.C.**—A plague, described in detail by the Athenian writer Thucydides, sweeps across the eastern Mediterranean and strikes Athens three times at the height of the Pelopennesian War. From the description of the symptoms, some modern scientists have suggested that the plague may have been Ebola hemorrhagic fever.

**1976**—Ebola hemorrhagic fever is recognized as a new disease after it surfaces in Yambuku, Zaire. The outbreak kills 318 people.

**1976**—At the same time as the outbreak in Zaire, a different strain of Ebola appears in Nzara and Maridi, Sudan, and in the surrounding area. Again, it is spread mainly through close personal contact within hospitals. Deaths total 284.

**1976**—Ebola shows up outside of Africa for the first time; a laboratory technician in England is infected after an accidental stick with a contaminated needle. He survives; no one else is infected.

**1979**—Ebola-Sudan reappears in Nzara, Sudan, killing thirty-four people.

**1989**—Monkeys in quarantine facilities in Virginia, Texas, and Pennsylvania begin dying of Ebola, which is apparently transmitted through the air. Several hundred monkeys are euthanized to stop the spread of the disease. Four humans develop antibodies to the virus, indicating that they were infected with it, but do not become ill. The new strain, which apparently affects monkeys but not humans, is called Ebola-Reston after Reston, Virginia, where it was first identified.

**1990**—Ebola-Reston shows up again in monkeys imported from the Philippines into quarantine facilities in Virginia and Texas. Four humans develop antibodies but do not get sick.

**1992**—Monkeys from the Philippines imported into Sienna, Italy, are found to be infected with Ebola-Reston. No humans are infected.

**1994**—Richard Preston publishes the best-selling book *The Hot Zone*, which details the events surrounding the outbreak among the monkeys in Reston, Virginia, and raises the possibility that Ebola could produce a horrifying worldwide epidemic. The book single-handedly raises public awareness of and interest in Ebola to a fever pitch.

**1994**—An outbreak of Ebola-Zaire in gold-mining camps deep in the rain forest of Gabon kills forty-four people. It is originally thought to be yellow fever, and is not identified as Ebola hemorrhagic fever until 1995.

**1994**—A new strain of Ebola, Ebola-Ivory Coast, surfaces among wild chimpanzees in the Ivory Coast. One scientist becomes ill after conducting an autopsy on one of the chimpanzees; she is transported to Switzerland for treatment and recovers.

**1995**—The movie *Outbreak*, starring Dustin Hoffman, depicts an Ebola-like virus (but one that can be transmitted by air) loose in North America.

**1995**—A second major outbreak of Ebola-Zaire occurs in Kikwit, Democratic Republic of the Congo, and the surrounding area, and is traced to an individual who worked in the forest adjoining the city. The disease again spreads through families and hospitals. The outbreak garners worldwide media attention, due to the interest in Ebola sparked by *The Hot Zone* and *Outbreak*. The final death toll is 315.

1996—A chimpanzee found dead in the forest in the Mayibout area of Gabon is eaten by people looking for food. The chimpanzee was infected with Ebola-Zaire. Nineteen people involved in butchering the animal become ill, and pass the disease on to their family members. In all, thirty-seven people die.

1996—A dead chimpanzee found in the forest near the Booué area of Gabon leads to another outbreak of Ebola-Zaire, killing sixty people.

1996—A medical professional who treats Ebola patients travels from Gabon to Johannesburg, South Africa, where he becomes ill. Although he recovers, the nurse attending him dies.

1996—Monkeys from the Philippines bring Ebola-Reston into a quarantine facility in Texas. No humans are infected.

1996—Ebola-Reston is found in a monkey export facility in the Philippines. No humans are infected.

1997—Dr. Gary Nabel and colleagues report development of an apparently effective vaccine against Ebola in guinea pigs.

2000—Dr. Gary Nabel and colleagues report development of an apparently effective vaccine that works in monkeys.

2001—The process of arranging to test the vaccine for safety in humans begins.

2000 —An outbreak of Ebola-Sudan in the Gulu, Masindi,
–2001 and Mbarara districts of Uganda kills 425 people. The three most important risks associated with infection are attending funerals of patients, family contact, and providing medical care to Ebola patients without using adequate protective measures.

# Glossary

**antibiotics**—Drugs that kill bacteria inside the body.

**antibodies**—Proteins produced by the immune system in response to an infection.

**antiseptic**—A substance that prevents or stops the growth of microorganisms.

**autopsy**—Examination of body organs and tissues after death.

**bacteria**—A self-contained microscopic organism that eats, excretes, and reproduces—and sometimes causes disease.

**biohazard**—A biological agent or condition that constitutes a hazard to humans or the environment.

**biosafety**—Safety with respect to the effects of biological research on humans and the environment.

**bodily fluids**—Any fluids produced by the body (blood, sweat, urine, and saliva are examples.

**cell**—The fundamental unit of all organisms; the smallest structural unit capable of independent functioning.

**cell culture**—Cells grown in a test tube or other laboratory device for experimental purposes. These cells can be infected with a virus in order to grow more copies of the virus.

**chloroquine**—A drug used to treat malaria.

**cremate**—To dispose of a dead body by burning.

**deoxyribonucleic acid (DNA)**—A substance that encodes genetic information in the nucleus of cells. It determines the structure, function, and behavior of the cell.

**diagnosis**—The process by which a doctor determines what disease a patient is suffering from.

**diarrhea**—The frequent evacuation of abnormally liquid feces.

**electron microscope**—An instrument that focuses a beam of electrons, instead of light, to produce an enlarged image of objects too small to be seen with an ordinary microscope.

**ELISA**—Enzyme-linked immunosorbent assay. In ELISA tests, a sample of an unknown virus is added to an enzyme that reacts chemically to only one specific virus. In the presence of the right virus, the enzyme turns a specific color.

**embalm**—To treat a dead body to protect it from decay.

**endothelial cells**—Specialized cells that line blood vessels in the body.

**epidemiology**—The study of epidemics.

**euthanize**—To kill humanely; to "put to sleep."

**feces**—The solid waste produced by animals' digestive tracts.

**filoviruses**—A type of virus that looks like a worm under the electron microscope. The four strains of Ebola and the one known strain of Marburg are the only known species of filoviruses.

**gene**—The basic unit of heredity; a section of DNA coding for a particular trait.

**genome**—The complete genetic material of an organism.

**immune system**—A system of cells that protects a person from bacteria, viruses, toxins, and other foreign substances.

**index case**—The first person to develop symptoms at the start of an outbreak of disease.

**influenza**—A respiratory infection, caused by a virus, that can also produce muscle aches, fever, chills, and nausea. Commonly called "the flu."

**interferon**—A compound produced by the immune system to kill virus-infected cells before they can spew more viruses into the system.

**malaria**—A tropical disease carried by mosquitoes that causes fever and chills.

**Marburg hemorrhagic fever**—A viral hemorrhagic fever, similar to Ebola, caused by a filovirus.

**microbiologist**—A scientist who studies microscopic life forms, such as bacteria and viruses.

**mutation**—A change in the genetic makeup of an organism.

**nausea**—A feeling of being sick to the stomach.

**nonhuman primates**—Monkeys and chimpanzees. Humans are also classified as primates.

**nosocomial**—Originating or taking place in a hospital.

**pathogenesis**—The origination and development of a disease.

**pathology**—The study of the changes produced by disease.

**polymerase chain reaction (PCR)**—A method of replicating genetic material.

**proteins**—The complex type of molecules out of which living tissue is formed.

**quarantine**—To keep an infected or potentially infected person or animal separate from other people or animals to prevent the possible transmission of disease.

**RNA**—Ribonucleic acid, the genetic material of the Ebola virus.

**shigella**—A common African bacteria-caused disease that results in bloody diarrhea.

**tissue**—A group of similar cells that act together in the performance of a particular function.

**virus**—An organism that is unable to reproduce on its own. Instead, it invades living cells and tricks them into producing hundreds of new viruses, which spill out when the cell dies and bursts.

# For More Information

## Organizations

Centers for Disease Control and Prevention
1600 Clifton Road
Atlanta, GA 30333
(404) 639-3534
(800) 311-3435
http://www.cdc.gov

World Health Organization
Avenue Appia 20
1211 Geneva 27
Switzerland
(+00 41 22) 791 21 11
e-mail: info@who.int
http://www.who.org

# Chapter Notes

## Chapter 1. A Terrifying Killer

1. Ed Regis, *Virus Ground Zero: Stalking the Killer Viruses With the Centers for Disease Control and Prevention* (New York: Pocket Books, 1996), pp. 107–109.

2. Michael Balter, "Emerging Diseases: On the Trail of Ebola and Marburg Viruses," *Science*, November 3, 2000.

3. "Ebola Hemorrhagic Fever Fact Sheet," Centers for Disease Control and Prevention Web site, n.d. <http://www.cdc.gov/ncidod/dvrd/spb/mnpages/dispages/ebola.htm> (September 18, 2001).

4. Ibid.

5. Ibid.

6. Ibid.

7. "Ebola Hemorrhagic Fever: Table Showing Known Cases and Outbreaks, in Chronological Order," Centers for Disease Control and Prevention Web site, n.d. <http://www.cdc.gov/ncidod/dvrd/spb/mnpages/dispages/ebotabl.htm> (September 18, 2001).

8. "Ebola Hemorrhagic Fever Fact Sheet."

9. Ibid.

10. Ibid.

## Chapter 2. The History of Ebola

1. Nancy Emond, "The Plague in Athens During the Pelopennesian War," The Asclepion Web site, n.d. <http://www.indiana.edu/~ancmed/plague.htm> (September 25, 2001).

2. P. E. Olson, M.D., C. S. Hames, M.D., A. S. Benenson, M.D., E. N. Genovese, Ph.D., "The Thucydides Syndrome: Ebola Déjà vu? (or Ebola Reemergent?)," *Emerging Infectious Diseases*, Vol. 2, No. 2, April–June 1996, Letters.

3. Ibid.

4. "Plague of Athens: Another medical mystery solved at University of Maryland," University of Maryland press release, January 1999, <http:///www.umm.edu/news/releases/athens.html> (September 25, 2001).

5. "Ebola Hemorrhagic Fever: Table Showing Known Cases and Outbreaks, in Chronological Order," Centers for Disease Control and Prevention Web site, n.d. <http://www.cdc.gov/ncidod/dvrd/spb/mnpages/dispages/ebotabl.htm> (September 18, 2001).

6. Tara Waterman, "Ebola Zaire Outbreaks," Tara's Ebola Site (Honors Thesis, Stanford University), n.d. <http://www.stanford.edu/group/virus/filo/eboz.html> (September 17, 2001).

7. Ed Regis, *Virus Ground Zero: Stalking the Killer Viruses With the Centers for Disease Control and Prevention* (New York: Pocket Books, 1996), p. 109.

8. Ellen Wallace, "In His Words: Africa's Deadly Visitor: Terror Imitates Art as the Killer Ebola Virus Makes Another Lethal Appearance," *People Magazine*, May 29, 1995.

9. Sean Henahan, "Dr. Frederick A. Murphy Talks About the Ebola Virus," Access Excellence Web site, n.d. <http://www.accessexcellence.org/WN/NM/interview_murphy.html> (November 22, 2000).

10. Tara Waterman, "Ebola Sudan Outbreaks," Tara's Ebola Site (Honors Thesis, Stanford University), n.d. <http://www.stanford.edu/group/virus/filo/ebos.html> (September 25, 2001).

11. "Ebola Hemorrhagic Fever: Table Showing Known Cases and Outbreaks, in Chronological Order."

12. "Ebola Sudan Outbreaks."

13. Tara Waterman, "Ebola Reston Outbreaks," Tara's Ebola Site (Honors Thesis, Stanford University), n.d. <http://www.stanford.edu/group/virus/filo/ebor.html> (September 25, 2001).

14. "Ebola Hemorrhagic Fever Fact Sheet," Centers for Disease Control and Prevention Web site, n.d. <http://www.cdc.gov/ncidod/dvrd/spb/mnpages/dispages/ebola.htm> (September 18, 2001).

15. Tara Waterman, "Ebola Côte d'Ivoire Outbreaks," Tara's Ebola Site (Honors Thesis, Stanford University), n.d. <http://www.stanford.edu/group/virus/filo/eboci.html> (September 25, 2001).

16. Ed Regis, *Virus Ground Zero: Stalking the Killer Viruses With the Centers for Disease Control and Prevention* (New York: Pocket Books, 1996), p. 235.

17. Ibid., pp. 148–149.

18. Ibid., pp. 157–159.

19. Ibid., p. 149.

20. Ibid., p. 151.

21. Ibid., p. 153.

22. "Ebola Hemorrhagic Fever: Table Showing Known Cases and Outbreaks, in Chronological Order."

23. Ibid.

24. Ibid.

25. Reuters, "Study: Protein key to Ebola effects," MSNBC Web site, n.d. <http://www.msnbc.com/news/440043.asp> (November 22, 2000).

26. Stefan Lovgren and Catherine Roberts, "World: Mysterious Killer: Virus hunters from around the world battle to contain a deadly outbreak of Ebola," *Maclean's*, November 13, 2000, p. 42.

27. "Outbreak of Ebola Hemorrhagic Fever, Uganda, August 2000–January 2001," Canada Communicable Disease Report, Vol. 27–06, March 15, 2001, <http://www.hc-sc.gc.ca/hpb/lcdc/publicat/ccdr/01vol27/dr2706eb.html> (June 5, 2001).

28. "Ebola Hemorrhagic Fever: Table Showing Known Cases and Outbreaks, in Chronological Order."

29. Reuters, "Ebola may shut off immune defenses," MSNBC Web site, n.d. <http://www.msnbc.com/news/480383.asp> (October 24, 2000).

30. Fred Guterl and Shehnaz Suterwalla, "A New Weapon Against Ebola: A vaccine for monkeys holds out hope for people," *Newsweek*, November 12, 2000, p. 91.

## Chapter 3. What is Ebola Hemorrhagic Fever?

1. Ed Regis, *Virus Ground Zero: Stalking the Killer Viruses With the Centers for Disease Control and Prevention*, (New York: Pocket Books, 1996), pp. 60–61.

2. "Ebola Hemorrhagic Fever Fact Sheet," Centers for Disease Control and Prevention Web site, n.d. <http://www.cdc.gov/ncidod/dvrd/spb/mnpages/dispages/ebola.htm> (September 18, 2001).

3. Kenneth Cockwill, Leah Goin, and Bernadet Nitychoruk, "Filoviridae: Ebola and Marburg Viruses," n.d. <http://duke.usask.ca/~misra/virology/stud2001/filovirus/Filoviridae1.html> (September 20, 2001).

4. Regis, p. 103.

5. Ibid.

6. Ibid., p. 104.

7. Ibid.

## Chapter 4. Diagnosing Ebola Hemorrhagic Fever

1. Ed Regis, *Virus Ground Zero: Stalking the Killer Viruses With the Centers for Disease Control and Prevention*, (New York: Pocket Books, 1996), pp. 12–14.

2. Ibid., pp. 18–20.

3. Ibid., p. 20.

4. Ibid., p. 21.

5. Ibid., pp. 40–42.

6. Ibid., pp. 42–43.

7. Joshua Amupadhi, "Sharp-Witted Doctor Spotted Ebola in South Africa," *Africa News Service*, November 23, 1996.

8. "Virology and Molecular Diagnostics," Iowa State University College of Veterinary Medicine Veterinary Diagnostic Laboratory Web site, n.d. <http://www.vdpam.iastate.edu/VDL/MainMenu/ViroMole.htm#PCR> (October 6, 2001).

9. "Ebola Hemorrhagic Fever Fact Sheet," Centers for Disease Control and Prevention Web site, n.d. <http://www.cdc.gov/ncidod/dvrd/spb/mnpages/dispages/ebola.htm> (September 18, 2001).

## Chapter 5. Treatment of Ebola Hemorrhagic Fever

1. Marty Fisher, "The Disease Cowboy," Duke University Medical Center—Medical Alumni News Web site, <http://www2.mc.duke.edu/daa/man/sp99/man1_2.html> (August 17, 2001).

2. "Ebola Hemorrhagic Fever Fact Sheet," Centers for Disease Control and Prevention Web site, n.d. <http://www.cdc.gov/ncidod/dvrd/spb/mnpages/dispages/ebola.htm> (September 18, 2001).

3. Kenneth Cockwill, Leah Goin, and Bernadet Nitychoruk, "Treatment of Marburg and Ebola Viruses," Filoviridae: Ebola and Marburg Viruses Web site, n.d. <http://duke.usask.ca/~misra/virology/stud2001/filovirus/TREATMEN.htm> (September 20, 2001).

4. "Ebola Hemorrhagic Fever Fact Sheet."

5. "Treatment of Marburg and Ebola Viruses."

6. Phillip B. Iverson and Loren A. Will, "Ebola Hemorrhagic Fever," Iowa State University Veterinarian Web site, n.d. <http://www.vetmed.iastate.edu/isuvet/s97-1.html> (June 5, 2001).

7. Joshua Amupadhi, "Sharp-Witted Doctor Spotted Ebola in South Africa," *Africa News Service*, November 23, 1996.

## Chapter 6. Social Implications of Ebola Hemorrhagic Fever

1. Glenn McKenzie, Associated Press, "Terrifying mystique surrounds deadly Ebola disease in Africa: Some blame evil spirits for scourge that kills up to 80% of victims," *The Dallas Morning News*, April 10, 1998, p. 16A.

2. Simon Robinson-Gulu, "Letter From Uganda: A Trip Inside An African Hot Zone. What happens to a small town and its people when the Ebola virus erupts?", *Time*, October 30, 2000, p. 8.

3. McKenzie.

4. "A Return to Kikwit, Zaire—Birthplace of Ebola," *All Things Considered*, National Public Radio, September 2, 1996.

5. Ed Regis, *Virus Ground Zero: Stalking the Killer Viruses with the Centers for Disease Control and Prevention* (New York: Pocket Books, 1996), p. 153.

6. "A Return to Kikwit, Zaire—Birthplace of Ebola."

7. Ibid.

8. "Ebola battle claims a brave warrior," *The Toronto Star*, December 18, 2000.

9. "Ebola Kills Dr. Lukwiya," *Africa News Service*, December 6, 2000.

10. "Ebola battle claims a brave warrior."

11. Ibid.

12. "A Return to Kikwit, Zaire—Birthplace of Ebola."

13. Ibid.

14. Associated Press, "Ebola survivors face fear and rejection in Uganda," CNN Web site, n.d. <http://www.cnn.com/2000/WORLD/Africa/11/17/ebola.survivors.ap/> (November 22, 2000).

15. Ibid.

16. Michael Fumento, "Hysteria strain of Ebola fever," *The Washington Times*, February 8, 2001.

17. Leslie Papp, "The real outbreak has been . . . hype," *The Toronto Star*, February 10, 2001.

18. Ibid.

19. Fumento.

20. Papp.

21. Ibid.

22. John Schwartz, "A blur of fact, fiction—Hype surrounding Ebola outbreak has led to much misinformation," *Minneapolis Star Tribune*, May 15, 1995, p. 01A.

23. Richard Preston, *The Hot Zone* (New York: Anchor Books, 1994), p. 406.

24. Regis, p. 235.

25. Bert Lauwers, "Ebola is just a dumb macho virus, expert says," Reuters, May 9, 1996.

26. Ibid.

27. Ibid.

## Chapter 7. Preventing Ebola Hemorrhagic Fever

1. Ed Regis, *Virus Ground Zero: Stalking the Killer Viruses With the Centers for Disease Control and Prevention* (New York: Pocket Books, 1996), pp. 109–110.

2. Ibid., pp. 110–111.

3. "Notice to Readers Update: Management of Patients with Suspected Viral Hemorrhagic Fever—United States," *Morbidity and Mortality Weekly Report*, June 30, 1995, Vol. 44, No. 25, pp. 475–479.

4. Stefan Lovgren, "Virus hunters tracking Ebola," MSNBC Web site, n.d. <http://www.msnbc.com/news/481082. asp> (November 22, 2000).

5. Tara Waterman, "Could Bats Be Ebola's Natural Host/Reservoir?", Tara's Ebola Site (Honors Thesis, Stanford University), n.d. <http://www.stanford.edu/group/virus/filo/bats. html> (September 25, 2001).

6. Tara Waterman, "Are Plants Ebola's Natural Reservoir?" Tara's Ebola Site (Honors Thesis, Stanford University), n.d. <http://www. stanford.edu/group/virus/filo/plants.html> (September 25, 2001).

7. Tara Waterman, "Are Insects Ebola's Natural Host/Reservoir?", Tara's Ebola Site (Honors Thesis, Stanford University), n.d. <http://www.stanford.edu/group/virus/filo/insects. html> (September 25, 2001).

8. Laurie Garrett, "Search for Ebola/From leafhoppers to chimps: Key to viral outbreak may be chain of transmission," *Minneapolis Star Tribune*, October 9, 1996, p. 03A.

9. Ibid.

10. Ibid.

11. Ibid.

# Chapter 8. Research and Future Prospects

1. Ed Regis, *Virus Ground Zero: Stalking the Killer Viruses With the Centers for Disease Control and Prevention* (New York: Pocket Books, 1996), p. 198.

2. Ibid., pp. 200–201.

3. Ibid., p. 202.

4. Reuters, "Study: Protein key to Ebola effects," MSNBC Web site, July 31, 2000, <http://www.msnbc.com/news/440043.asp> (November 22, 2000).

5. Michael Balter, "EMERGING DISEASE: On the Trail of Ebola and Marburg Viruses," *Science*, November 3, 2000.

6. "Study: Protein key to Ebola effects."

7. Ibid.

8. Balter.

9. Reuters, "Ebola may shut off immune defenses," MSBNC Web site, October 23, 2000, <http://www.msnbc.com/news/480383.asp> (October 24, 2000).

10. Valerie Depraetere, "Ebola vaccine hope," *Nature Science Update*, November 30, 2000, <http://www.nature.com/nsu/nsu_pf/001130/001130-8.html> (October 10, 2001).

11. Associated Press, "Ebola virus gene offers hope for future vaccine: DNA injection protects guinea pigs in study," *The Dallas Morning News*, December 30, 1997, p. 3A.

12. Robin Eisner, "Vaccine Stops Ebola," ABCNEWS.com, November 29, 2000, <http://more.abcnews.go.com/sections/living/dailynews/ebolavaccine001129.html> (October 10, 2001).

13. Ibid.

14. "Ebola virus gene offers hope for future vaccine."

15. Eisner.

16. Ibid.

17. Dennis R. Burton and Paul W. H. I. Parren, "Fighting the Ebola virus," *Nature*, November 30, 2000, pp. 527–528.

# Further Reading

Day, Nancy. *Superbugs: The Story of Drug-Resistant Diseases.* Berkeley Heights, NJ: Enslow Publishers, Inc., 2001.

Draper, Allison Stark. *Ebola.* New York: Rosen Publishing, 2001.

Morse, Stephen S., ed. *Emerging Viruses.* New York: Rockefeller University, 1996.

Olshaker, Mark and C. J. Peters (Contributor). *Virus Hunter: Thirty Years of Battling Hot Viruses Around the World.* New York: Doubleday, 1998.

Olstone, Michael B. A. *Viruses, Plagues & History.* New York: Oxford University Press, 1998.

Preston, Richard. *The Hot Zone.* New York: Anchor Books, 1994.

Regis, Ed. *Virus Ground Zero: Stalking the Killer Viruses With the Centers for Disease Control and Prevention.* New York: Pocket Books, 1996.

Ryan, Frank. *Virus X: Tracking the New Killer Plagues.* New York: Little, Brown & Company, 1998.

# Internet Addresses

**The Centers for Disease Control and Prevention**
<http://www.cdc.gov>

**The World Health Organization**
<http://www.who.int/en/>

**The Big Picture Book of Viruses: Filoviridae**
<http://www.virology.net/Big_Virology/BVRNAfilo.html>

# Index

## M

Makokou, 55
malaria, 8, 17, 32, 36, 46, 57, 63, 71
Marburg virus, 18, 19, 33, 71, 78, 81, 82, 85
Martin, Mary Lane, 45, 46
Massika, Bernard, 55–56
Matshimoseka, Colette, 62
Mayinga, 69, 70
McCormick, Joe, 50–51, 53
measles, 16
Menga, Gaspar, 26
meningitis, 46
Minioko, Madar, 57–58, 60
Monath, Tom, 79–80
monkey, 20–22, 24, 31, 33, 35, 36, 64, 75, 85, 86, 87, 88
mosquito, 78
Mount Sinai School of Medicine, 30, 85
Murphy, Frederick A., 18, 81
Muyembe, Tamfum, 39–40

## N

Nabel, Gary, 29, 84, 86, 87, 88
National Institute for Virology, 47, 76
National Institute of Health (NIH), 84
*Nature*, 30, 86, 89
negative pressure, 72
*The New Yorker*, 64
Ngaliema Hospital, 67, 69
Nicol, Monsignor, 40
Northern Uganda, 32–33
nosocomial transmission, 13
Nzara, 50–51, 76

## O

Okot, Justin 32, 56
*Outbreak*, 64, 67
Owete, Esther, 32–33, 56

## P

Parren, Paul W. H. I., 89
Pasteur Institute, 24
Pelopennesian War, 15
Pericles, 15
Peters, C. J., 66, 81
Philippines, 11, 21, 22, 24, 35
Philipps Universitat, 30, 85
pig, 84, 85
Piot, Peter, 18
plague, 63, 67
pneumonia, 63
polymerase chain reaction (PCR), 48
Pont Mwembe forest, 26
Preston, Richard, 11, 21, 22, 64, 66, 67
primers, 48
*Proceedings of the National Academy of Sciences*, 85
protein, 85, 87

## R

reagent, 46
Red Cross, 60
reservoir, 20, 75–76, 78–79
retrovirus, 83
rheumatoid arthritis, 54
RNA virus, 33, 65
rodent, 88
Rollin, Pierre, 37, 38, 41, 42, 45, 81
Russia, 79, 82
Ryabchikova, Elena, 79

## S

salmonellosis, 36
Sanchez, Anthony, 81, 82, 83
Sandton Clinic, 46
The Scripps Research Institute, 89
shigella, 26
simian hemorrhagic fever (SHF), 21–22
Sona, Beatric, 61

South Africa, 29, 46, 47, 54, 58, 67, 69, 76
State Research Center of Virology, 79
Sudan , 9, 19, 23, 24, 29–30, 34, 35, 41, 50–51, 86
Switzerland, 24

**T**

Tai Forest, 76
Tai National Park, 24
Thucydides, 15, 16
Toronto General Hospital's Centre for Travel and Tropical Medicine, 63
tuberculosis bacteria, 43, 63
typhoid fever, 24, 36, 46, 47, 71
typhus fever, 24

**U**

Uganda, 11, 29–30, 35, 56, 58, 59, 61, 62, 75, 85
United States Army Medical Research Institute of Infectious Diseases (USAMRIID), 21–22, 88
University of Kinshasa, 39

U.S. National Institute of Health (NIH), 29

**V**

van der Groen, Guido, 41, 67, 68
van Mullem, Johan, 40
Van Nieuwenhove, Simon, 40, 41
viral hemorrhagic fever, 33, 71–72, 74, 79, 81
viral hepatitis, 36
*Virus*, 64
VP35, 85

**W**

Wilson, Mary, 65
World Health Organization, 17, 59, 64, 75, 79

**Y**

Yambuku, 7–8, 16–17, 18, 19, 39, 40, 41, 69
yellow fever, 18, 36

**Z**

Zaire, 9, 11, 18, 23, 24, 25–29, 34, 37, 39–40, 53, 67, 69, 79, 86, 87. *See also* Democratic Republic of the Congo.
Zimbabwe, 78